World Economic Situation and Prospects 2005

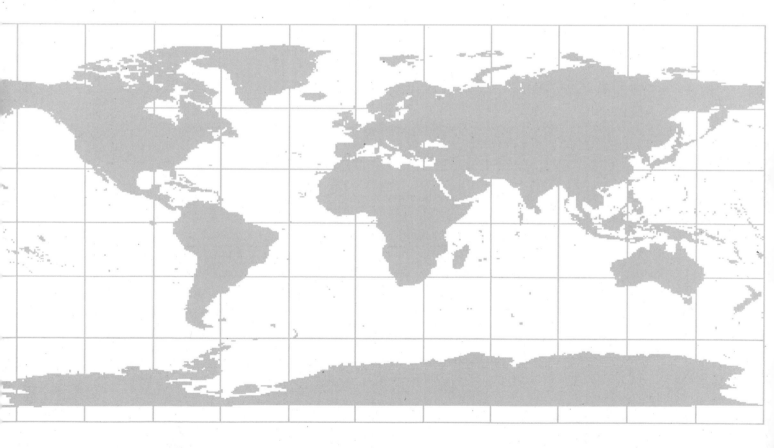

UnitedNations
NewY ork,2005

This report is a joint product of the Department of Economic and Social Affairs (DESA), the United Nations Conference on Trade and Development (UNCTAD) and the five United Nations regional commissions (Economic Commission for Africa (ECA), Economic Commission for Europe (ECE), Economic Commission for Latin America and the Caribbean (ECLAC), Economic and Social Commission for Asia and the Pacific (ESCAP), and Economic and Social Commission for Western Asia (ESCWA)). It provides an overview of recent global economic performance and short-term prospects for the world economy and of some key global economic policy and development issues. One of its purposes is to serve as a point of reference for discussions on economic, social and related issues taking place in various United Nations entities in the first half of 2005.

For further information, please contact:

In New York

Mr. José Antonio Ocampo
Under-Secretary-General
Department of Economic and Social Affairs
Room DC2-2320
United Nations, New York 10017
U.S.A.

Phone: (212) 963-5958
Fax: (212) 963-1010
E-mail: jaocampo@un.org

In Geneva

Mr. Carlos Fortin
Deputy Secretary-General
United Nations Conference on
 Trade and Development
Palais des Nations, Room E-9052
1211 Geneva 10
Switzerland

Phone: (41) (22) 907-5789
Fax: (41) (22) 907-0057
E-mail: carlos.fortin@unctad.org

Executive Summary

At the beginning of 2005, the cyclical recovery in the world economy was reaching its zenith; growth of gross world product (GWP) increased by 4 per cent in 2004, compared to 2.8 per cent in 2003 and a forecast of 3¼ per cent for 2005. Growth in the developing countries was the fastest for more than two decades, while output in the remaining economies in transition continued to increase more rapidly than in the other major country groups.

The world economy has considerable momentum entering 2005 and most determinants of the short-term prospects remain positive, with only a modest deceleration anticipated for 2005. The higher oil price has already slowed global growth somewhat and policy measures intended to avert overheating will reduce it further, including in the United States and China, the principle engines for the global economy at present. The growth of international trade will slow accordingly and the upward movement in the prices of oil and several other commodities is unlikely to continue, reducing that stimulus to many developing countries. The expected upward drift in interest rates will also cause growth to ease in many countries.

The high aggregate rate of growth in 2004 in part reflected the fact that the improvement was almost universal: every region except South Asia and the Commonwealth of Independent States (CIS) grew more rapidly in 2004 than in 2003. In these two exceptional cases, growth slipped from its previous high levels but remained above 6 per cent and 7 per cent, respectively. All the groups of countries with special development challenges—the least developed and landlocked countries and the small island developing States (SIDS)—grew by more than 5 per cent in 2004. On a per capita basis, output increased by more than 3 per cent in almost half the developing countries, but these countries accounted for over 80 per cent of the developing world's population. The widespread nature of growth in developing countries in 2004 was attributable to the fact that most countries benefited from one or more of three unusually coincidental developments: rapid growth of trade in manufactures, increased prices for oil and most non-oil commodities and calmer conditions in international financial markets.

Among the developed countries, performance was more varied. Growth was strong in North America, moderate in Japan but weak in Europe. With the exception of its new members and a few other countries, the European Union has replaced Japan as the lagging economy. A modest cyclical acceleration is expected in these slow-growing countries in 2005 but growth will still languish around 2 per cent.

One of the universal weaknesses in the world economy continues to be the slow growth of employment and the persistence of high rates of unemployment and underemployment in most developing countries. Unless improved economic growth is reflected in increased employment, it will prove difficult to reduce poverty. Even in the most rapidly growing region, East Asia, unemployment and underemployment remain problems in several economies. The need to absorb the millions of surplus workers in the agriculture sector and in State-owned enterprises in China is a special case, but lack of employment is also a problem in other countries in the region. In 2004, there were signs of an improving employment situation in Latin America; this increased employment should translate into increased domestic demand and thereby be sustained. More generally, domestic demand gained strength in many developing countries in 2004, pointing to the possibility of more general gains in employment if growth can be sustained. In the developed countries, employment is recovering slowly in the United States but continues to be weak in Europe and Japan so that the term "jobless growth" remains largely applicable.

The United States is increasingly being complemented in its role as the main engine of growth for the world economy by China. The combined strong demand from these two countries has provided a wide-ranging boost to global growth because China has acted as a catalyst in several areas of economic activity where the United States provides less stimulus. For example, with manufacturing playing a less important role in its economy, growth in the United States has a limited impact on the demand for raw materials but larger implications for trade in manufactured goods. Increasing Chinese demand for raw materials to fuel its industrial expansion, on the other hand, has been an important factor in reversing, at least temporarily, the long-term downward trend in the prices of non-oil commodities, thereby improving the formerly weak prospects of countries exporting such products. The index of non-oil commodity prices in dollars rose by a further 10 per cent in 2004, following gains of over 11 per cent in 2003 and almost 12 per cent in 2002. These improvements in part reflected the concurrent depreciation of the dollar. Moreover, they followed a lengthy period of declining prices: the average dollar prices of non-oil commodities were about 25 per cent lower at the end of 2004 than in 1980.

Oil prices rose by over 50 per cent in the first part of 2004, mainly because of the persistent increase in demand. This contrasted with the oil crises of the 1970s, when record prices were the result of reduced supplies from the major producers. Following the latest surge, prices fell back towards the end of 2004 and are expected to ease further with the moderation in the growth of the world economy. However, since the supply of oil is unlikely to be able to respond to the underlying growth of demand in the medium term, oil prices are not expected to retreat to their 2003 levels for any extended period in the near future.

The world economy accommodated this rapid shift to a new oil price regime in 2004 without major disruption. In the developed countries, core inflation did not increase untowardly. Among the developing countries vulnerable to an oil price shock, the effects were muted for those producing minerals and metals by the increased prices they received for their exports. The impact of the higher oil prices is expected to continue to be limited in 2005, although there remains the possibility that non-economic factors could severely disrupt the international oil market, to the detriment of global economic growth. Even without a major shock, oil markets are such that prices are likely to remain volatile.

In contrast with commodity markets, international capital markets remained calm in 2004, having to address only the remnants of former financial crises rather than new ones. Flows of foreign direct investment (FDI) to developing countries reversed their three-year downward trend and there were instances of successful bond issuances by developing countries as yield spreads narrowed over the course of the year. Flows of official development assistance (ODA) began to reflect earlier increases in commitments, although part of the increase was for international security and emergency relief rather than for development spending. Total net financial flows to developing countries declined from 2003 levels, primarily because of scheduled repayments under multilateral financial institution lending programmes. In addition to scheduled debt payments by the majority, a few developing countries were able to restructure or reduce their private sector external debt while others increased their foreign exchange reserves, sometimes substantially.

The overall outcome of the various financial flows was a seventh consecutive year of a net transfer of resources out of developing countries, at a record level of $300 billion in 2004. Except for sub-Saharan Africa, all developing regions, as well as the economies in transition, experienced a negative net transfer. However, some of this net transfer reflected positive rather than negative developments: as a result of strong growth in export revenues, some countries had trade surpluses which they chose to use as a means to improve their self-insurance against possible balance-of-payments difficulties, either by increasing their foreign exchange reserves or by reducing their foreign debt. The perceived need for such self-insurance must be seen as a major deficiency of the international financial system.

These increases in foreign exchange reserves were a partial reflection of the global external imbalances which not only persisted but increased in 2004. The largest of these imbalances was the United States trade deficit which rose to more than $650 billion, or above 5 per cent of GDP. This was countered by surpluses in a number of Asian developing countries, Japan and the European Union (EU). These imbalances were one of the forces causing the exchange rate of the dollar to continue its three-year decline and to reach a new low against the euro in 2004.

Apart from the depreciation of the dollar, the global imbalances failed to have significant repercussions in 2004, but the possibility of an abrupt and globally damaging correction persists since a depreciation of the dollar alone seems unlikely to be sufficient to reduce the global imbalances to sustainable levels in an orderly fashion. At the same time, efforts to correct the imbalances should not focus only on the deficit countries or regions because such an approach is likely to be excessively contractionary. In the present case, some correction of the United States fiscal deficit and an improvement in its private savings rate seems indispensable, but the contractionary effect of such action should be counterbalanced by expansionary measures elsewhere. It is necessary to ensure that global growth and stability are sustained.

Countries with external surpluses will therefore need to stimulate domestic demand, preferably investment in physical and social infrastructure. If such additional investment is deemed unnecessary, resources could be channelled to developing countries with unmet investment needs. As an immediate requirement, the extensive reconstruction required following the tsunami of December 2004 calls for an increase in investment within the Asian region.

These domestic actions should be complemented by various forms of enhanced international cooperation. In order to make sure that global growth is not derailed, cooperation is necessary to ensure coherence among national policy actions to address the imbalances. Improved cooperation in exchange-rate policy among the major developed countries and with the leading developing economies in Asia should be used to devise a phased and non-disruptive approach to any necessary changes in exchange-rate regimes.

All these actions should be such that they also contribute to the longer-term global development agenda, most notably the attainment of the Millennium Development Goals by 2015. Progress is being made in increasing ODA, but the total is only around one third of the target of 0.7 per cent of the gross national income (GNI) of the developed countries and falls far short of the amount deemed necessary to achieve the Millennium Development Goals. Further progress in raising ODA needs to be accompanied by enhanced debt relief for all developing countries that are confronted with unsustainable external debt burdens and by further progress on measures to prevent and resolve financial crises. Finally, for the benefit of all countries, but with the primary objective of improving the development prospects of developing countries, it is also necessary to ensure the equitable completion of the programme of multilateral trade negotiations agreed at Doha.

The overall agenda is challenging but universally recognized. All members of the international community should rededicate themselves to the task at the summit meeting of the General Assembly in September 2005.

Contents

Annex:

Boxes

Figures

Tables

Explanatory Notes

The following symbols have been used in the tables throughout the report:

..   **Two dots** indicate that data are not available or are not separately reported.

–   **A dash** indicates that the amount is nil or negligible.

-   **A hyphen (-)** indicates that the item is not applicable.

-   **A minus sign (-)** indicates deficit or decrease, except as indicated.

.   **A full stop (.)** is used to indicate decimals.

/   **A slash (/)** between years indicates a crop year or financial year, for example, 1990/91.

-   **Use of a hyphen (-)** between years, for example, 1990-1991, signifies the full period involved, including the beginning and end years.

Reference to **"dollars" ($)** indicates United States dollars, unless otherwise stated.

Reference to **"tons"** indicates metric tons, unless otherwise stated.

Annual rates of growth or change, unless otherwise stated, refer to annual compound rates.

In most cases, the growth rate forecasts for 2004 and 2005 are rounded to the nearest quarter of a percentage point.

Details and percentages in tables do not necessarily add to totals, because of rounding.

The following abbreviations have been used:

AGOA	African Growth and Opportunity Act (United States)
ASEAN	Association of Southeast Asian Nations
ATC	Agreement on Textiles and Clothing
AU	African Union
BIT	bilateral investment treaty
bpd	barrels per day
BTA	bilateral trade agreement
CAC	collective action clause

CCL	Contingent Credit Line (IMF)
CFA	Communauté financière africaine
CIS	Commonwealth of Independent States
CPI	consumer price index
CRTA	Committee on Regional Trade Agreements (WTO)
DAC	Development Assistance Committee (of OECD)
DTT	double taxation treaty
EBA	"Everything But Arms" (EU)
EBRD	European Bank for Reconstruction and Development
ECA	Economic Commission for Africa
ECB	European Central Bank
ECE	Economic Commission for Europe
ECLAC	Economic Commission for Latin America and the Caribbean
ESCAP	Economic and Social Commission for Asia and the Pacific
ESCWA	Economic and Social Commission for Western Asia
ESM	Emergency Safeguard Measures (GATS)
EU	European Union
FAO	Food and Agriculture Organization of the United Nations
FASB	United States Accounting Standards Board
FATF	Financial Action Task Force (Bretton Woods institutions)
FDI	foreign direct investment
Fed	United States Federal Reserve
FSAP	Financial Sector Assessment Programme (IMF)
FSF	Financial Stability Forum
FTA	free trade agreement
GATS	General Agreement on Trade in Services
GATT	General Agreement on Tariffs and Trade
GDP	gross domestic product
GNI	gross national income
GNP	gross national product

GSP	Generalized System of Preferences	**NYMEX**	New York Mercantile Exchange
GWP	gross world product	**ODA**	official development assistance
HICP	Harmonized Index of Consumer Prices	**OECD**	Organization for Economic Cooperation and Development
HIPC	heavily indebted poor countries		
IASB	International Accounting Standards Board	**OPEC**	Organization of the Petroleum Exporting Countries
IBRD	International Bank for Reconstruction and Development	**pb**	per barrel
		PPP	purchasing power parity
ICAC	International Cotton Advisory Committee	**PRGF**	Poverty Reduction and Growth Facility (IMF)
ICO	International Coffee Organization	**Project LINK**	international collaborative research group for econometric modelling, coordinated jointly by the Economic Monitoring and Assessment Unit of the United Nations Secretariat, and the University of Toronto
ICT	information and communication technologies		
IDA	International Development Association		
IF	Integrated Framework for Trade-related Technical Assistance for the Least Developed Countries		
		PRSPs	Poverty Reduction Strategy Papers (IMF and World Bank)
IFAC	International Federation of Accountants	**PTA**	preferential trade agreement
IFC	International Finance Corporation	**R&D**	research and development
IFRS	International Financial Reporting Standards	**ROSCs**	Reports on the Observance of Standards and Codes (Bretton Woods institutions)
IMF	International Monetary Fund		
IT	information technology	**RTA**	regional trade agreement
ITCB	International Textiles and Clothing Bureau	**SARS**	severe acute respiratory syndrome
JITAP	Joint Integrated Technical Assistance Programme	**SDT**	special and differential treatment
LDCs	least developed countries	**SGP**	Stability and Growth Pact
Liffe	London International Financial Futures and Options Exchange	**SIDS**	small island developing States
		SOEs	State-owned enterprises
LME	London Metal Exchange	**TNCs**	transnational corporations
M&As	mergers and acquisitions	**UN/DESA**	Department of Economic and Social Affairs of the United Nations Secretariat
mbd	millions of barrels per day		
MCA	Millennium Challenge Account (United States)	**UNCITRAL**	United Nations Commission on International Trade Law
MCC	Millennium Challenge Corporation (United States)		
MFA	Multifibre Arrangement	**UNCTAD**	United Nations Conference on Trade and Development
MT	metric tons		
NAMA	non-agricultural market access	**UNU**	United Nations University
NNP	net national product	**VERS**	voluntary export restraints
NPV	net present value	**WIDER**	World Institute for Development Economics Research (UNU)
NTB	non-tariff barriers		
NYBOT	New York Board of Trade	**WTO**	World Trade Organization

The designations employed and the presentation of the material in this publication do not imply the expression of any opinion whatsoever on the part of the United Nations Secretariat concerning the legal status of any country, territory, city or area or of its authorities, or concerning the delimitation of its frontiers or boundaries.

The term "country" as used in the text of this report also refers, as appropriate, to territories or areas.

For analytical purposes, the following country groupings and sub-groupings have been used:

Developed economies (developed market economies):
Europe, excluding the European transition economies
Canada and the United States of America
Japan, Australia and New Zealand.

Major developed economies (the Group of Seven):
Canada, France, Germany, Italy, Japan, United Kingdom of Great Britain and Northern Ireland, United States of America.

European Union:
Austria, Belgium, Cyprus, Czech Republic, Denmark, Estonia, Finland, France, Germany, Greece, Hungary, Ireland, Italy, Latvia, Lithuania, Luxembourg, Malta, Netherlands, Poland, Portugal, Slovakia, Slovenia, Spain, Sweden, United Kingdom of Great Britain and Northern Ireland.

Economies in transition:

Southern and Eastern Europe
Albania, Bulgaria, Croatia, Romania, Serbia and Montenegro, The former Yugoslav Republic of Macedonia.

Commonwealth of Independent States (CIS)
Armenia, Azerbaijan, Belarus, Georgia, Kazakhstan, Kyrgyzstan, Republic of Moldova, Russian Federation, Tajikistan, Turkmenistan, Ukraine, Uzbekistan.

Developing economies:
Africa
Asia and the Pacific (excluding Japan, Australia, New Zealand and the member States of CIS in Asia).
Latin America and the Caribbean.

Subgroupings of Asia and the Pacific:

Western Asia:
Bahrain, Iraq, Israel, Jordan, Kuwait, Lebanon, Oman, Qatar, Saudi Arabia, Syrian Arab Republic, Turkey, United Arab Emirates, Yemen.

East and South Asia:
All other developing economies in Asia and the Pacific (including China, unless listed separately). This group has in some cases been subdivided into:

China

South Asia: Bangladesh, India, Iran (Islamic Republic of), Nepal, Pakistan, Sri Lanka.

East Asia: all other developing economies in Asia and the Pacific.

Subgrouping of Africa:

Sub-Saharan Africa, excluding Nigeria and South Africa (commonly contracted to "sub-Saharan Africa"):
All of Africa except Algeria, Egypt, Libyan Arab Jamahiriya, Morocco, Nigeria, South Africa, Tunisia.

For particular analyses, developing countries have been subdivided into the following groups:

Oil-exporting countries:
Algeria, Angola, Bahrain, Bolivia, Brunei Darussalam, Cameroon, Colombia, Congo, Ecuador, Egypt, Gabon, Indonesia, Iran (Islamic Republic of), Iraq, Kuwait, Libyan Arab Jamahiriya, Mexico, Nigeria, Oman, Qatar, Saudi Arabia, Syrian Arab Republic, Trinidad and Tobago, United Arab Emirates, Venezuela, Viet Nam.

Oil-importing countries:
All other developing countries.

Least developed countries:
Afghanistan, Angola, Bangladesh, Benin, Bhutan, Burkina Faso, Burundi, Cambodia, Cape Verde, Central African Republic, Chad, Comoros, Democratic Republic of the Congo, Djibouti, Equatorial Guinea, Eritrea, Ethiopia, Gambia, Guinea, Guinea-Bissau, Haiti, Kiribati, Lao People's Democratic Republic, Lesotho, Liberia, Madagascar, Malawi, Maldives, Mali, Mauritania, Mozambique, Myanmar, Nepal, Niger, Rwanda, Samoa, Sao Tome and Principe, Senegal, Sierra Leone, Solomon Islands, Somalia, Sudan, Timor-Leste, Togo, Tuvalu, Uganda, United Republic of Tanzania, Vanuatu, Yemen, Zambia.

Landlocked developing countries:
Afghanistan, Armenia, Azerbaijan, Bhutan, Bolivia, Botswana, Burkina Faso, Burundi, Central African Republic, Chad, Ethiopia, Kazakhstan, Kyrgyzstan, Lao People's Democratic Republic, Lesotho, Malawi, Mali, Mongolia, Nepal, Niger, Paraguay, Rwanda, Swaziland, Tajikistan, The former Yugoslav Republic of Macedonia, Turkmenistan, Uganda, Uzbekistan, Zambia, Zimbabwe.

Small island developing States:
Antigua and Barbuda, Bahamas, Bahrain, Barbados, Belize, Cape Verde, Comoros, Cook Islands, Cuba, Cyprus, Dominica, Dominican Republic, Fiji, Grenada, Guinea-Bissau, Guyana, Haiti, Jamaica, Kiribati, Maldives, Malta, Marshall Islands, Mauritius, Micronesia (Federated States of), Nauru, Niue, Palau, Papua New Guinea, Saint Kitts and Nevis, Saint Lucia, Samoa, Sao Tome and Principe, Seychelles, Singapore, Solomon Islands, Saint Vincent and the Grenadines, Suriname, Tonga, Trinidad and Tobago, Tuvalu, Vanuatu.

Heavily Indebted Poor Countries:
Angola, Benin, Bolivia, Burkina Faso, Burundi, Cameroon, Central African Republic, Chad, Comoros, Congo, Côte d'Ivoire, Democratic Republic of the Congo, Ethiopia, Gambia, Ghana, Guinea, Guinea-Bissau, Guyana, Honduras, Kenya, Lao People's Democratic Republic, Liberia, Madagascar, Malawi, Mali, Mauritania, Mozambique, Myanmar, Nicaragua, Niger, Rwanda, Sao Tome and Principe, Senegal, Sierra Leone, Somalia, Sudan, Togo, Uganda, United Republic of Tanzania, Viet Nam, Zambia.

The designation of country groups in the text and the tables is intended solely for statistical or analytical convenience and does not necessarily express a judgement about the stage reached by a particular country or area in the development process.

Chapter I
Global outlook

With no major shocks, global economic growth is expected to slow to 3¼ per cent in 2005, following an increase of 4 per cent in 2004 (see table I.1). World economic activity continues to follow a largely cyclical pattern, with a strong upturn in late 2003 and the first half of 2004 resulting in some major economies moving closer to full capacity utilization. This has given rise to a number of developments that are likely to cause global growth to slow towards its current longer-term potential.

> Higher global growth in 2004 will moderate in 2005

With recovery having been secured in most countries, policy stimuli are being gradually withdrawn, amplifying the deceleration. Monetary policy is being slowly tightened worldwide. Many countries, including several of the largest, have fiscal deficits that are widely regarded as excessive; efforts to reduce them will have a moderating effect on growth. These policy actions will be particularly pertinent in the United States, dampening growth in that country and reducing the impetus that it has provided as one of the engines of growth for the world economy. Elsewhere, actions have been taken to bring the economic expansion in China to a more sustainable rate, although the anticipated deceleration is modest. Finally, high global growth has manifested itself in increased prices for oil and many other commodities. Experience shows that the net effect of higher oil prices is a reduction in global growth but developments in 2003 and 2004 suggest that higher non-oil commodity prices may, on balance, have a positive effect on global demand (see below).

Despite these downward pressures, underlying global economic conditions remain sound and global growth is expected to moderate, not to suffer a reversal. The immediate challenge facing policy makers is to achieve the maximum long-term sustainable rate of growth without precipitating overheating or some other form of reversal. Over the longer term, the task is to raise the maximum sustainable rate of growth, particularly in the poorest countries and regions where it is lagging.

The world economy weathered a number of largely unanticipated and potentially adverse economic shocks in 2004, as well as the tsunami in Asia at the end of the year, whereas some major potential threats to global economic stability failed to materialize. The largest economic shock was the increase in oil prices by almost 60 per cent in the first ten months, before easing towards the end of the year. A second shock was the continuing change in exchange rates among the major currencies, with the euro and yen appreciating by a further 14 per cent and 11 per cent, respectively, against the dollar between May and December. Thirdly, the prices of many non-oil commodities increased in 2004, albeit not to the extent of oil prices.

> Economic shocks had only a limited impact in 2004

These three shocks had partially offsetting effects for most countries: often, one or two shocks had adverse effects but the other(s) were beneficial. For example, the impact of higher dollar oil prices was countered by currency appreciation against the dollar in some cases and, for non-oil commodity producing countries, by higher prices for their exports. Higher non-oil commodity prices largely involve a transfer of resources to poor countries which are likely to have a higher propensity to consume than many of the importing countries. Moreover, none of the three shocks caused the respective prices to hit new records: the real price of oil did not reach its level of the 1970s, the improvement in non-oil commodity prices did little to make up for the downward trend since 1980 (see figure I.1) and the value of the dollar, in terms of the other major currencies or in trade-weighted terms,

Table I.1.
Growth of world output and trade, 1995-2005

	Annual percentage change										
	1995	1996	1997	1998	1999	2000	2001	2002	2003[a]	2004[b]	2005[b]
World output[c]	2.8	3.4	3.7	2.4	3.1	4.0	1.3	1.9	2.8	4.0	3¼
of which:											
Developed economies	2.4	2.9	3.3	2.6	3.0	3.5	1.0	1.4	2.2	3.4	2½
North America	2.5	3.6	4.5	4.2	4.5	3.8	0.6	2.3	3.0	4.1	3
Western Europe	2.5	1.8	2.6	2.9	2.8	3.5	1.6	1.1	1.1	2.3	2¼
Asia and Oceania[d]	2.0	3.5	2.0	-0.7	0.5	2.8	0.6	0.0	2.5	3.6	2
Economies in transition	-3.3	-2.5	0.9	-3.3	3.9	8.3	5.7	5.0	7.0	7.1	6
Southern and Eastern Europe	7.3	2.9	-1.0	0.2	-2.3	3.7	5.0	4.8	4.2	5.8	4¾
Commonwealth of Independent States	-5.2	-3.7	1.4	-4.0	5.4	9.3	5.9	5.1	7.6	7.3	6
Developing economies	4.7	5.8	5.4	2.0	3.6	5.7	2.4	3.4	4.6	6.2	5½
Africa	3.1	5.3	3.4	3.0	3.1	3.3	3.4	3.1	4.0	4.5	4¾
East Asia	8.6	7.7	6.5	0.4	6.4	7.7	3.8	6.1	6.0	7.2	6½
South Asia	6.0	5.9	4.5	4.9	5.5	5.2	4.7	4.5	6.7	6.3	6¼
Western Asia	4.1	4.9	4.1	2.7	-0.7	5.5	-1.3	2.5	5.0	5.5	4½
Latin America and the Caribbean	0.5	3.9	5.3	2.4	1.1	4.1	0.5	-0.4	1.7	5.4	4
Other groupings											
Landlocked developing countries	0.6	4.1	4.0	2.6	3.5	4.2	5.0	4.4	4.0	5.9	5¾
Least developed countries	5.5	5.7	5.0	4.5	4.5	4.7	5.1	4.9	4.1	5.2	5½
Small island developing States	5.8	5.9	5.3	1.9	5.5	7.7	0.3	2.2	1.7	5.3	4½
Sub-Saharan Africa	4.9	5.8	4.4	4.0	3.1	2.6	3.3	3.6	2.9	5.5	5¾
Memo item:											
World trade	8.6	5.5	9.2	3.3	5.2	11.5	-0.9	2.5	6.2	10.6	8
World output growth with PPP-based weights[e]	3.5	4.0	4.2	2.6	3.6	4.6	2.3	2.8	3.8	5.0	4¼

Source: Department of Economic and Social Affairs of the United Nations Secretariat (UN/DESA).

a   Partly estimated.

b   Forecasts, based in part on Project LINK, an international collaborative research group for econometric modelling, coordinated jointly by the Economic Monitoring and Assessment Unit of the United Nations Secretariat, and the University of Toronto.

c   Calculated as a weighted average of individual country growth rates of gross domestic product (GDP), where weights are based on GDP in 2000 prices and exchange rates.

d   Japan, Australia and New Zealand.

e   Employing an alternative scheme for weighting national growth rates of GDP, based on purchasing power parity (PPP) conversions of national currency GDP into international dollars (see introduction to annex: statistical tables).

Figure I.1.
Non-fuel commodity price indices, 1970-2003 (2000 = 100)

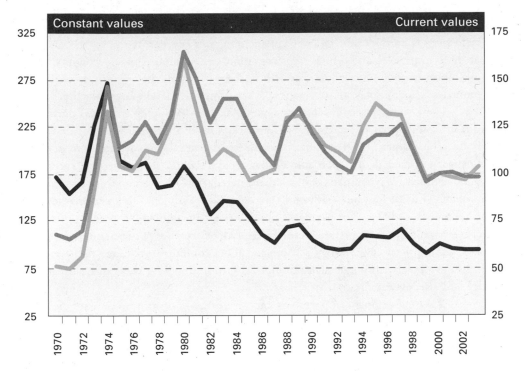

Current SDR

Current US dollar

Real terms[a]

Sources:
UNCTAD, *Monthly Commodity Price Bulletin;* UN/DESA, *Monthly Bulletin of Statistics.*

a   Non-fuel commodity price indices deflated by manufacture price index.

remained above earlier lows. Despite offsetting effects and their limited magnitude, the achievement of high and widespread economic growth in the context of these changes in a number of key international prices suggests an increased ability and capacity to accommodate such shocks. In particular, the shocks had few immediate second-round effects, such as transmission into accelerating inflation and consequent pressure to tighten domestic policies. An improved degree of macroeconomic stability in most countries, both developed and developing, were one reason for increased resilience to the shocks.

Although confronted with these unforeseen shocks, the world economy did not encounter the full impact of the major downside risks that were identified at the beginning of 2004. Continued security concerns were among the factors that affected the price of oil, but otherwise fears of major new adverse geopolitical developments failed to materialize during the year. Similarly, there was no major international economic disruption as a result of the prevailing global imbalances. The dollar depreciated substantially, but with no major disturbances to financial markets or national economies. The forecast for 2005 assumes that these downside risks will have no more bearing on the global economic outcome than they did in 2004. Nevertheless, these risks, particularly those posed by the global imbalances, persist and remain a potential vulnerability. It cannot be assumed that the outcome will necessarily be so benign in the future.

International trade expanded with the growth for the world economy as a whole in 2004, increasing by more than 10 per cent during the year (see table A.7). The trade of developing countries grew more rapidly than that of the developed countries, mostly because of China and India. The growth of international trade is expected to slow to 8 per cent in 2005, in tandem with the deceleration in overall economic growth. A more

Some broader downside risks failed to materialize in 2004 but some will persist in 2005

The acceleration in international trade in 2004 will moderate in 2005

substantial slowdown, for example, because of a setback in one of the major importing countries, would have correspondingly adverse effects for the world economy at large.

With no new financial crises in 2004, lending conditions improved for those countries with access to international financial markets. Despite a temporary mid-year setback, yield spreads for the sovereign bonds of emerging markets narrowed over the course of the year, reflecting the financial markets' recognition of the sounder macroeconomic situation and improved domestic economic growth in these countries. Low returns in the developed countries also prompted greater interest in investment in developing countries.

There were successful bond issuances by a few developing countries during the year and, for a somewhat larger group of countries, a reversal of the three-year decline in foreign direct investment (FDI) flows. Nevertheless, the net supply of capital to developing countries declined in 2004 because of net repayments of debt. In some cases, this involved scheduled repayments of earlier crisis-related and other loans from the international financial institutions but, with more favourable conditions in financial markets and diminished needs for balance-of-payments financing, a few countries were in a position to reduce and restructure their private sector external debt. For the poorest countries, previous increases in official development assistance (ODA) commitments began to be translated into disbursements, although such resources continue to fall far short of needs in both quantity and effectiveness in most instances.

When other financial payments and receipts are taken into account, the result was the seventh consecutive year of an increasing net transfer of resources out of developing countries, to a record level of over $300 billion. Except for sub-Saharan Africa (where the transfer was almost nil), all developing regions, as well as the economies in transition, experienced a negative net transfer.

A negative net transfer may comprise both negative and positive elements. In the past, it has often reflected the need to use domestic resources in order to make payments on external debt and other foreign liabilities, thus involving a compression of domestic demand and a slowdown in economic growth. On this occasion, part of the negative net transfer had more positive connotations for many developing countries: it reflected strong domestic growth and the fact that export revenues exceeded import expenditures; this allowed the countries concerned to use their surpluses either to reduce their foreign debt or to accumulate foreign reserves as a precaution against future balance-of-payments difficulties.

The global external imbalances widened further in 2004, with the United States merchandise trade deficit increasing from some $550 billion in 2003 to more than $650 billion, or above 5 per cent of gross domestic product (GDP). Both price and quantity effects contributed to the deterioration. Because the determinants of United States trade flows are unlikely to change in the short term, the country's trade balance is projected to widen further in 2005 and beyond unless there is a change in policy or a major market correction.

Reacting to the positive development of improved global economic growth and the negative development of a burgeoning United States external imbalance (see below), foreign exchange markets were volatile in 2004, with a continuation of the three-year downward trend in the value of the dollar punctuated by periodic, but partial, rebounds. Overall, the dollar reached new lows against the euro (see figure I.2). Forces pushing the dollar down included the United States current-account deficit, fed in part by the fiscal deficit, periodic worries over the durability of the United States recovery and portfolio rebalancing by international investors, with euro-denominated holdings being increased as a share of total assets

Conditions for developing countries in international capital markets improved but net capital flows remained low...

... and there was a record negative net transfer of financial resources

The global external imbalances widened in 2004, with little improvement in sight

The dollar fell to its lowest level against the euro

Figure I.2.
Exchange rates: Euro/US dollar and Yen/US dollar, 1998-2005

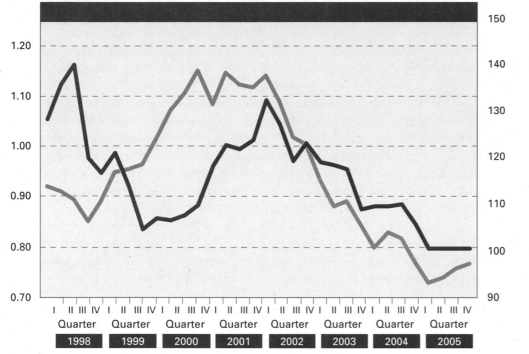

Euro/US dollar

Yen/US dollar

Source:
UN/DESA, based on Project LINK.

to diversify risk. However, there remained countervailing pressures in the form of stronger growth in the United States compared to both the euro zone and Japan, the narrowing and then reversal of interest rate differentials between the United States and the euro zone, and intervention by the Bank of Japan (BoJ) in foreign currency markets in an effort to dampen the yen's appreciation. These opposing forces resulted in occasional brief appreciation of the dollar against the backdrop of decline, but the seemingly intractable nature of the United States twin deficits suggests continuing dollar weakness. The present forecast is based on the assumption that the exchange rates among the major currencies will stabilize at approximately the levels prevailing at the beginning of 2005 but, for reasons explored below, there is a risk that the dollar will decline further. This could pose difficulties for all other countries, notably those whose currencies float against the dollar.

Assuming its countercyclical role, macroeconomic policy stimulus was reduced as the recovery gained momentum in 2004. In the first instance, many central banks began to raise interest rates, gradually reversing the monetary easing that they had adopted following the slowdown in 2001. Nevertheless, the process was incremental since policy makers recognized the fragility of the recovery in some countries. In the United States, for example, the Federal Reserve (Fed) raised the Federal Funds rate five times in the second half of 2004, albeit by a total of only 125 basis points. The exceptions to the upward trend were the BoJ and the European Central Bank (ECB), as the recovery in these economies was regarded as weak and growth as below potential. Since interest rates are still at historical lows, the tightening initiated in some countries is expected to continue in 2005. However, the BoJ is expected to maintain its zero-interest rate in 2005, while the ECB will have to decide whether to delay tightening monetary policy if the appreciation of the euro threatens the recovery or if the recovery otherwise continues to be weak.

Policy stimulus is being reduced in many developed countries

Monetary policy in
most developing
countries will remain
broadly
accommodative

The direction of monetary policy in developing economies in 2004 was mixed. Some countries tightened policy modestly in response to emerging inflationary pressures while a few other economies, such as the Republic of Korea, Hungary, South Africa and Turkey, reduced interest rates, because of either weakening growth, currency appreciation or, despite higher oil and commodity prices, diminished inflationary pressures. Unless there is a supply-side shock that raises inflation substantially, such as a further surge in oil prices, monetary policy in 2005 is expected to remain generally accommodative in most developing countries across all regions.

Globally, domestic
demand is becoming
an increasingly
important source of
growth

Domestic demand assumed an increasingly important source of improved growth in 2004 and contributed to the dynamism of international trade. Personal incomes have risen in many countries and, notwithstanding the continuing overarching global threats, consumer and business confidence has improved; private sector expenditure has risen accordingly. Greater macroeconomic stability has removed some uncertainty and contributed to improved private sector confidence, especially in a number of developing countries and economies in transition. In some key developed countries and a number of the more rapidly growing developing countries, however, the strengthening of consumer demand has been fuelled not by higher incomes but by increases in wealth in the form of higher asset prices, notably of housing but also of financial assets, and, in some cases, consumer debt. These sources of support to consumer demand are susceptible to setbacks, particularly in the face of higher interest rates.

The tsunami will have
only a limited impact
on short-run growth

The human toll and physical destruction of the tsunami in Asia at the end of December 2004 was unprecedented and will have human, social, environmental and developmental repercussions for years to come. From a short-term economic perspective, however, the impact will be less extensive. Output from the affected areas will be reduced, but there will be an offsetting boost from relief and reconstruction activities. Experience from lesser environmental disasters suggests that, with the necessary international support, economic recovery can be rapid so that, despite the magnitude of the disaster, it is expected to have only a limited impact on short-term growth, possibly reducing it by up to half a percentage point in the most affected countries.

Some key aspects of growth in 2004

Improved global
growth was
widespread

Global economic growth in 2004 was not only the highest for many years, but also unusually widespread and well balanced. All but two of the major regional groupings of countries achieved higher growth than in 2003. In the exceptional cases of the Commonwealth of Independent States (CIS) and South Asia, growth nevertheless remained above 7 per cent and 6 per cent, respectively. Even the higher price of oil did not have the discriminating effects that might have been assumed. In Latin America, with its large number of oil-importing countries, growth surged to over 5 per cent after six years of weak performance. In Africa, the impact of higher oil prices was offset for many oil-importing countries by higher non-oil commodity prices; non-oil prices rose less than oil prices, but non-oil commodities often accounted for a higher proportion of exports than oil did of imports. For its part, Asia, despite also being predominantly an oil-importing region, received an even greater stimulus than other regions from the rapid growth in China and the large increase in trade that it generated.

The broadening of the recovery in 2004 is reflected in the fact that almost half the developing countries, accounting for over 80 per cent of the developing world's population, increased per capita output by more than 3 per cent (see table I.2). Per capita output also increased by more than 3 per cent in all the economies in transition except one.

Output per capita rose by more than 3 per cent in almost half the developing countries in 2004

Table I.2.

Frequency of high and low growth of per capita output, 2002-2004

	Number of countries monitored	Decline in GDP per capita			Growth of GDP per capita exceeding 3 per cent		
		2002	2003	2004[a]	2002	2003	2004[a]
		Number of countries					
World	159	38	31	13	45	56	78
of which:							
Developed economies	33	2	3	0	7	7	10
Economies in transition	19	1	0	0	16	15	18
Developing countries	107	35	28	13	22	34	50
of which:							
Africa	51	15	14	9	10	15	21
East Asia	13	1	2	1	7	5	10
South Asia	6	1	0	0	2	4	5
Western Asia	13	7	4	2	2	6	6
Latin America	24	11	8	1	1	4	8
Memo items:							
Least developed countries	41	13	12	8	10	11	20
Sub-Saharan Africa	31	9	9	6	8	8	13
Landlocked developing countries	26	7	6	3	10	10	14
Small Island developing States	17	6	7	2	1	5	5
	Share[b]	Percentage of world population					
Developed economies	15.5	2.1	1.6	0.0	0.6	0.6	2.8
Economies in transition	5.6	0.1	0.0	0.0	4.9	4.7	5.3
Developing countries	78.9	8.1	10.2	2.3	34.3	55.7	64.7
of which:							
Africa	13.2	2.3	3.0	1.1	2.4	5.3	5.5
East Asia	31.0	0.1	0.9	0.8	28.9	27.2	29.7
South Asia	23.4	0.4	0.0	0.0	1.5	20.8	23.4
Western Asia	2.8	1.3	0.8	0.3	1.1	1.6	1.6
Latin America	8.5	4.0	5.5	0.1	0.4	0.8	4.5
Memo items:							
Least developed countries	10.7	2.0	2.9	1.5	3.2	4.5	7.4
Sub-Saharan Africa	7.7	1.9	2.7	0.8	2.4	2.1	4.6
Landlocked developing countries	4.9	1.2	1.9	0.4	1.4	1.2	2.9
Small Island developing states	0.8	0.3	0.4	0.2	0.0	0.1	0.1

Source: UN/DESA, including population estimates and projections from *World Population Prospects: The 2000 Revision vol. I, Comprehensive Tables* and corrigendum (United Nations publication, Sales No. E.01.XIII.8 and Corr. 1).

a   Partly estimated.
b   Percentage of world population for 2000.

Of the 107 developing countries for which data are available, per capita output fell in only 13 cases, and these countries accounted for less than 3 per cent of the population. Of these 13 countries, nine were in Africa and accounted for almost one quarter of that region's population. On the other hand, almost half the countries in Africa (but accounting for only 40 per cent of the region's population) increased per capita output by more than 3 per cent. Nevertheless, these cases demonstrate that it is possible to achieve rates of growth in Africa that, if sustained, will slowly reduce poverty in the region. In South and East Asia, only four countries, accounting for less than 3 per cent of the region's population, failed to achieve 3 per cent growth of per capita output in 2004. In Western Asia, two of the four countries that experienced a decline in per capita output in 2003 achieved positive growth in 2004, but only half the countries in the region—the same number as in 2003—increased per capita output by more than 3 per cent. By these measures, the largest turnaround in 2004 was in Latin America: in 2003, one third of the 24 countries in the region for which data are available (accounting for over 60 per cent of the region's population) experienced a decline in per capita output; in 2004, the same number of countries, accounting for over half the region's population, increased per capita output by more than 3 per cent.

Some limited gains in employment finally appear in developing countries

The expansion of employment in developing countries has been lacklustre in recent years. Preliminary evidence suggests some improvement in 2004, but generating additional employment, particularly for lower skilled workers, remains a global challenge. Even in rapidly growing East Asia, unemployment and underemployment remain problems in several economies, but notably in such lower-income countries as Indonesia and the Philippines. In absolute terms, however, the problem remains the greatest in China where the restructuring and privatization of State-owned enterprises has converted a large amount of underemployment into unemployment. An economic slowdown in China would be to the detriment of the world economy, but those most adversely affected would be the millions of poor and unemployed in China itself. In the meantime, China's demand for raw materials contributed to the overall economic improvement in developing countries in 2004. In Latin America, for example, after several years of stagnation, this gave rise to some growth in employment. The resulting stimulus to domestic demand should help to consolidate these gains.

Despite the increase in oil revenues in Western Asia, the lag between increased public receipts from oil and their expenditure meant that employment gains were limited in 2004, but should improve from 2005 as new public programmes are initiated. Because of its heavy dependence on migrant labour, increased employment in the region has a beneficial impact, albeit modest, on labour markets elsewhere, notably in South and East Asia.

Data are not available on recent developments in labour markets in Africa, but improved growth in 2004 gives grounds for limited and cautious optimism against a backdrop of chronic structural unemployment and underemployment. Increased demand, as well as higher prices, for many of the region's commodity exports and the opening of some new trading opportunities under the European Union's (EU) "Everything But Arms" (EBA) initiative and the United States African Growth and Opportunity Act (AGOA) should have generated increased employment, albeit on a scale that is limited in relation to the magnitude of the problem.

In developed countries, the spectre of jobless growth has not yet disappeared

In the developed countries, labour markets have languished despite the recovery, leading some observers to coin the term "jobless recovery". In the United States, modest increases in the employment situation finally began to improve as 2004 progressed but the rate of unemployment remains well above the levels of the late 1990s. In contrast with the United

States, employment in Western Europe did not decline during the slowdown, but stopped increasing in 2003, and has picked up only marginally since. In Japan, unemployment has fallen gradually since the beginning of 2003. In most of these countries, however, the situation is worse than the data indicate because the unemployment figures do not include unemployed workers who have ceased looking for work because of the weak labour market.

Regional performance and outlook

The *United States* continues to be one of the main drivers of global economic growth. Its recovery continued in the first half of 2004 but slowed briefly at mid-year as consumer spending softened and exports stalled. However, there was a rebound in the third quarter and GDP for 2004 as a whole is estimated to have grown by at least 4 per cent. Consumer spending remains strong, business investment and productivity are increasing and inflation is low. Nevertheless, with interest rates moving up, fiscal stimuli waning, oil prices remaining at their increased levels and employment showing a hesitant recovery, growth in 2005 is expected to decelerate to 3 per cent.

> Strong growth in the United States is expected to moderate ...

The economic recovery in *Japan* appears to be losing momentum. Growth of domestic demand increased in early 2004 but then retreated. Reflecting the economy's continued reliance on the external sector, prospects for 2005 depend heavily on growth in China and the United States, oil prices and the global information and communication technologies (ICT) cycle, with a further appreciation of the yen posing a downside risk. The financial system is strengthening and deflation seems likely to be overcome by the end of 2005. Monetary policy remains accommodative, but the structural fiscal deficit is around 6 per cent of GDP and fiscal policy remains restrictive, with a proposal that some earlier tax cuts should be reversed.

> ... as is the resurgence in Japan

Despite the further appreciation of their currencies and their heavy reliance on the external sector, growth in *Australia, Canada,* and *New Zealand* accelerated in 2004. Canada is expected to sustain growth of almost 3 per cent in 2005, while some moderation is expected in Australia and New Zealand. Unemployment in the latter two economies has fallen to record lows, but inflation increased and both also have external deficits of around 5 per cent of GDP.

> Growth in Australia, Canada and New Zealand remains strong

Growth in *Western Europe* decelerated in the second half of 2004, partially as a result of higher oil prices. Growth for the year as a whole was 2.3 per cent and no improvement is expected in 2005. With the appreciation of the euro, exports, the major source of growth, have weakened, while consumer spending has remained lacklustre as a result of weaknesses and uncertainties in the labour market; business investment has shown more strength. Some improvement in employment and hence consumer demand is expected in 2005. Anticipating a recovery and, in some cases, the need to reduce deficits below the ceiling in the Stability and Growth Pact, fiscal policy is generally becoming more restrictive. Monetary policy in the euro area, on the other hand, is on hold as policy makers judge the persistence of the deceleration in the second half of the year and the consequences of the appreciation of the euro. Being more advanced in its recovery, the United Kingdom of Great Britain and Northern Ireland is a contrasting case, with policy interest rates having been raised in 2004 and some further increase expected in 2005.

> Limited improvement in growth is foreseen for Western Europe

In contrast with the sluggishness in the EU-15, growth in the eight *new EU members* from Central and Eastern Europe accelerated to 5 per cent in 2004 but peaked around mid-year so that some slowdown is expected in 2005. The reduced trade barriers associated with EU membership contributed to improved export growth, but domestic

> The new members of the European Union continue to grow strongly

demand was also strong in most cases, stimulating imports. However, the improved growth had little impact on employment whereas EU accession had some one-time inflationary effects, reinforced by higher energy prices. Macroeconomic policies remain largely supportive of growth, but structural fiscal deficits are large and some fiscal tightening is expected in 2005. Nevertheless, economic growth is expected to be maintained, although slower growth in the EU or higher energy prices would damage prospects.

Commodity-driven
growth in the CIS will
moderate in 2005

Largely as a result of increased commodity exports, but supported by strong domestic demand, growth in the *Commonwealth of Independent States* (CIS) exceeded 7 per cent in 2004, but there were signs of deceleration as the year progressed and these are expected to carry over into 2005. Employment increased but the total number of unemployed remains around 10 million, about 8 per cent of the labour force. Inflation continued to decline during the year but remained high in some countries; there were also signs of larger price increases in the future and anti-inflationary measures are likely to be adopted in some countries. Despite the strong growth, macroeconomic policy has been expansionary, in addition to which symptoms of "Dutch disease" have begun to emerge in some of the oil-exporting countries.

Growth in Africa
improves but remains
inadequate

GDP in *Africa* grew by 4.5 per cent in 2004, the largest increase in a decade. The sources of this improvement were higher demand and prices for Africa's exports, increased agricultural output, improved political stability and strengthened macroeconomic management in most countries, and continued donor support. These same factors are expected to produce a similar outcome in 2005. Only three countries suffered economic contraction in 2004, while six grew by the 7 per cent that is deemed a benchmark for the attainment of the Millennium Development Goals in the region. The prices of all but three of Africa's export commodities rose in 2004, thanks to which eight oil-producing countries, six other countries and the region as a whole achieved a current-account surplus. Further reducing the region's foreign exchange constraint, five additional countries received full heavily indebted poor countries (HIPC) debt relief during the year.

Oil-importing countries
share Western Asia's
benefits from higher
oil prices

The impediments to growth created by the geopolitical difficulties in *Western Asia* were countered in 2004 by the increase in oil prices. Regional output increased by over 5 per cent, with oil-importing countries performing better than oil-exporting countries, since many of the latter were already encountering capacity constraints. The oil-importing countries not only weathered the increase in oil prices and the continued difficulties associated with the situation in Iraq, but benefited from such regional spillover effects as remittances, financial flows, trade and tourism. Higher expenditures from oil revenues are already causing inflation to increase in the oil-exporting countries, while having a negligible impact on employment, particularly of nationals in each country. Growth in the region is expected to decelerate to 4½ per cent in 2005.

South Asia sustains
strong growth
despite setbacks

Poor weather caused growth in *South Asia* to slip in 2004, but it nevertheless remained above 6 per cent and is expected to sustain a similar rate in 2005, despite the year-end tsunami damage. With the setback to agriculture, growth originated mostly in the manufacturing and services sectors, in most cases being driven by both domestic and export demand. Export growth is expected to slow in 2005, with the expiry of the Agreement on Textiles and Clothing (ATC) being a mixed blessing to the individual countries of the region. Increased oil and non-oil commodity prices caused some acceleration of inflation in 2004 and further increases are expected in 2005, causing a tightening of monetary policies in some cases. Fiscal policies, in contrast, continue to be expansionary and, while slightly reduced in 2004, fiscal deficits remain high.

East Asia continued to be the most rapidly growing developing region in 2004, largely driven by China's growth of 9.2 per cent and the consequent expansion of intraregional trade. At the same time, domestic demand for manufactured goods is increasing in importance as higher incomes translate into increased consumption. This should provide the region with a degree of resilience to any moderation in China's import demand as a result of efforts to cool that economy. Higher oil prices narrowed external surpluses in 2004 and contributed to an acceleration in inflation; price pressures are expected to persist in 2005. Reflecting the high degree of globalization of the region, the prospects for 2005 will be subject to slower growth worldwide, the deceleration in China and higher oil prices. Growth in China is forecast to fall to 8¾ per cent, with that for the region as a whole slipping to 6½ per cent.

> Chinese growth plays a key role in East Asia

Growth in *Latin America and the Caribbean* reached 5.5 per cent in 2004, breaking a six-year period of very weak growth. The recoveries in Argentina and Venezuela and a marked improvement in Brazil accounted for much of the growth, but three other large countries also grew by more than 3 per cent and only one country—Haiti—suffered a decline in output. Exports, particularly of commodities, served as a catalyst to stimulate investment, and consumption responded to the consequent increase in employment. Higher export revenue also resulted in a second consecutive year of current-account surplus, allowing some countries to reduce their external debt. Similarly, higher tax receipts increased primary fiscal surpluses and some countries used the opportunity to reduce public debt. Growth in 2005 will remain heavily dependent on the external environment which is expected to be less stimulatory. Unusually, however, this may be offset by stronger domestic demand, particularly in the larger economies. Domestic demand is supported by sound macroeconomic conditions, as well as by some degree of employment and wage growth. Overall, growth is expected to be around 4 per cent in 2005, but remains subject to external risks. As elsewhere, higher oil prices or slower growth globally or in China would damage growth prospects, but the region is also subject to the additional risk of higher international interest rates.

> Latin America breaks out of its low growth

The 2004 oil price shock in perspective

Although prices had subsided by year's end, the surge in oil prices in 2004 triggered two main concerns: first, the risk of another global oil crisis which, according to some analysts, would dwarf the crises of the 1970s (both of which wreaked havoc on the world economy) and, second, the possibility of permanently higher oil prices in the long run. Despite their surge in 2004, oil prices in inflation-adjusted terms remained far below the record levels they reached in the late 1970s (see figure I.3); even the volatility in prices was less than in previous oil crises.

> The surge in oil prices resurrects short- and long-term concerns

Global oil production capacity was tight in 2004, exacerbated by various heightened uncertainties about supplies from some major oil-producing areas. Nevertheless, the rise in oil prices was driven mainly by strong global oil demand, not by reductions in supply, as was the case in past oil crises. On this occasion, the increased oil prices will lead to slower global economic growth in 2005 and beyond, but not necessarily to a substantial downturn or a recession. In particular, as long as there is no large-scale disruption in the global oil supply, an oil crisis of the type experienced at the beginning of the 1970s can be averted. The higher prices will gradually curb global oil demand and encourage new oil production, causing prices to retreat somewhat.

> Prices were driven higher by increased demand, rather than reduced supply

Figure I.3.
Oil prices: 1970-2004 (constant 2003 US dollars)

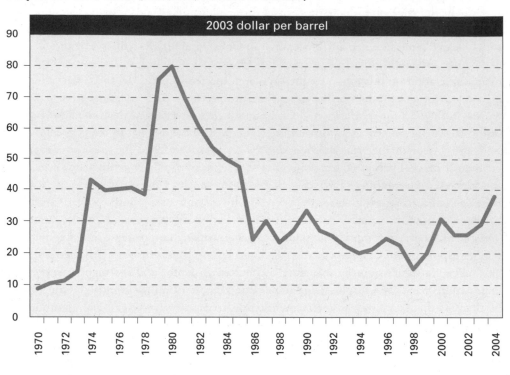

Sources:
BP Statistical Review of World
Energy, and UN/DESA estimate
for 2004 data.

The volatility of oil prices

The nature of the oil market makes prices inherently volatile

In addition to their general upward trend, oil prices were volatile in 2004. Oil prices tend to be volatile for a number of reasons. First, the price elasticity of global oil demand is low because oil is indispensable for many economic activities and possible substitutes for it are limited in the short run. Secondly, the income elasticity of global oil demand is high, also reflecting the close relationship between economic activity and the demand for energy. Thirdly, the price elasticity of oil supply is low in the short run because of both the long investment cycle in oil production and the oligopoly in the supply of oil.

Global oil demand is determined primarily by the strength of global economic activity

In the longer run, competition among oil producers, including the non-compliance of members of the Organization of the Petroleum Exporting Countries (OPEC) with their production quotas, limits the power of OPEC over the global oil market and increases the response of total oil supply to a sustained change in the price of oil. On balance, therefore, global oil demand is determined primarily by the strength of global economic activity and is influenced only marginally by fluctuations in oil prices, particularly in the short-to-medium term. For the same reasons, small changes in the balance between global oil demand and supply are likely to cause large fluctuations in oil prices. In the extreme cases of the past oil crises, disruptions in the global oil supply caused steep price increases.

Large movements in oil prices are usually followed by some correction

Experience suggests that it is not in the self-interest of oil suppliers to seek substantially higher oil prices because such higher prices derail global economic growth and this subsequently leads to a collapse in oil prices. Movements in oil prices can, however, be caused and greatly amplified by factors other than the actions of suppliers, such as geopolitical uncertainties about global oil supply and speculative behaviour in the oil market, particularly in the futures market. In the latter respect, oil prices can be subject to the "herd instinct" and similar behaviour that causes overshooting and bubbles in financial markets. The increased uncertainties prevailing for much of 2004 attracted additional speculative activity in the oil market and may have exacerbated the inherent volatility.

Macroeconomic effects of higher oil prices

Time-series studies suggest that the macroeconomic effects of increases in oil prices have diminished since the oil crises of the 1970s. Some also show that the negative impact of higher oil prices on real economic activity is likely to be limited to the short run, although the impact on inflation could last longer in some countries.[1] For their part, large-scale models provide numerical estimates of the impact of changes in oil prices on the incomes of oil producers and oil consumers, inflation, financial markets, business and consumer confidence, business costs, policy actions and international transmission mechanisms.

Higher oil prices dampen global growth ...

The initial impact of changes in oil prices is through the transfer of income. Higher oil prices transfer income from consumers to oil producers and, at the international level, from oil-importing countries to oil-exporting countries. For most oil-importing countries, higher oil prices lead to a reduction in their demand for imports of other goods and services unless they are able to draw on foreign reserves or foreign lending to mitigate the situation. On the other hand, the income gains lead to higher expenditure in the oil-exporting countries, but these countries usually do not spend all their gains immediately. The increase in spending by the oil-exporting countries is therefore likely to be less than the decrease in spending by oil-importing countries, leading to a decline in world aggregate demand, especially in the short run. It is this net decrease in global demand that ultimately reduces the demand for and price of oil.

... initially by reducing global aggregate demand

Higher oil prices increase costs in almost all industries, but particularly in such energy-intensive sectors as transport. Businesses will normally try to pass on their higher costs by raising the prices of their products. Higher oil prices are therefore likely to lead to an increase in inflation, the severity of which will depend, inter alia, on the extent to which companies pass on higher oil prices in the prices of their final products, on the consequences for wages and on the effectiveness of anti-inflationary policies.

Higher oil prices increase many other prices ...

The impact of higher oil prices on income, business profits and inflation—and the corresponding change in macroeconomic policies—is likely to lower the values of financial assets, which will affect the real economy through negative wealth effects and decreases in business investment. The two oil crises of the 1970s produced a major erosion of consumer and business confidence; in the United States, the corresponding indices plummeted 50 per cent, which led to further reductions in household consumption and business capital spending.

... and erode confidence

Both fiscal and monetary policies have a strong bearing on the macroeconomic impact of higher oil prices. Views are split over the efficacy of macroeconomic policies in handling the initial impact, but policy, notably monetary policy, is particularly relevant in determining the secondary effects and the process of recovery from an oil shock. Because of the magnitude of oil's role in the economy, particularly in the developed countries, higher oil prices will increase the inflation rate, causing the authorities to tighten monetary policy. In the cases of the previous oil shocks, many analysts believed that the adoption of restrictive policy measures in reaction to the inflationary effects of higher oil prices had far more far-reaching negative consequences than the other repercussions. With the reduced

Policy responses are likely to have further contractionary effects

oil intensity of the developed economies, the inflationary impact of higher oil prices, and hence the need for a tightening of monetary policy, will be less.

The negative repercussions are transmitted through international markets ...

Most of the first-round negative effects of higher oil prices on individual economies are likely to be amplified by changes in the terms of trade and changes in international trade and capital flows. After the initial income effects, the economic slowdown in oil-importing countries reduces their import demand and initiates a downward spiral of decreasing aggregate demand in the world economy. Similarly, a tightening of macroeconomic policies, especially a rise in interest rates in major developed economies, would have an impact on global financial markets. This would aggravate the external financial situation of developing countries, particularly low-income oil-importing countries with heavy foreign debt burdens and precarious balance-of-payments situations. On the other hand, international transmissions can also ameliorate the adverse impact of higher oil prices, for example through the recycling of the increased oil revenues of the oil-exporting countries to the rest of the world.

... resulting in a slowdown in global growth

Simulations of the impacts of an increase in oil prices suggest that a 20 per cent increase in oil prices would lead to an annual loss of gross world product (GWP) of 0.2-0.3 percentage points.[2] The estimates for individual countries and regions vary, but not by a large margin. For example, the loss in the GDP for the developed countries as a group is estimated to be about 0.3 per cent. Among developing countries, the impact would be the largest for oil-importing sub-Saharan African countries, with a loss of GDP of more than one percentage point, since imports of oil account for more than 10 per cent of GDP in some of these countries. These countries would suffer a reduction in domestic demand if there were no additional external financial resources to compensate for the higher oil bill. For Asian developing countries, the impact would be a loss of GDP in the range of 0.4-0.5 percentage points for China and India and even more for a few of the newly industrialized economies in Asia where oil intensity now surpasses that in the developed economies. The impact on most oil-importing economies in Latin America would be slightly less than in Asia. Studies also show that most oil-exporting countries would gain 5 percentage points or more in growth of their GDP.

Two cases of higher oil prices

A lacuna in most quantitative studies is the lack of a distinction between the case of higher oil prices mainly driven by strong oil demand, as in the current situation, and the case of higher oil prices caused predominantly by a reduction in oil supply, as in the oil crises of the 1970s and 1980s when production was reduced by a large margin.

Higher prices can be driven by reductions in supply or increases in demand

When higher oil prices are caused by a notable curtailment in supply, the physical shortage of oil leads to a direct disruption in overall economic activity, the lay-off of workers and welfare losses from higher oil prices. In contrast, when higher oil prices are caused mainly by stronger-than-anticipated demand, it is an indication that global economic growth is at or beyond the rate that can be supported by prevailing global oil production capacity. In both cases, there will be an income transfer from oil consumers to oil producers and from oil-importing countries to oil-exporting countries. However, in the case of a demand shock, part of the transfer is a redistribution of the strong global growth among the different parties in the oil-market; in this situation, the negative income effects should be small. In the case of a supply shock, the transfer has negative income effects for the global economy as a whole.

Both cases have distributional effects among countries and among income groups within countries: poor oil-importing countries and the low-income group within an oil-importing country will always be the most vulnerable to higher oil prices. In the case of a demand shock, the negative impact of higher oil prices on many oil-importing countries may be ameliorated by other factors, such as strong global demand for their exports of other commodities. Additional external financial resources would also help these countries to offset the adverse impact of higher oil prices. Within a country, increased fiscal transfers to the poor would reduce the burden of higher oil prices on lower-income groups.

Most developed economies have lowered their oil intensity (defined as primary oil consumed per unit of GDP) because they have become more energy-efficient in both production and consumption and because oil energy-intensive manufacturing activity accounts for a smaller proportion of their GDP than previously. Some of this manufacturing has moved to developing countries as part of the global integration of production and trade. When the final products reach developed countries as imports, the impact of higher oil prices on the final prices of these goods is marginal. Developed economies have therefore become less vulnerable to oil shocks, but the situation is the opposite for many oil-importing developing countries.

The oil-intensity of production has declined in developed countries ...

These assertions may, however, be more valid in the case of a demand-driven increase in oil prices than in the case of an oil supply shock. Lower oil intensity gives most developed countries an advantage only if higher oil prices are driven by strong global demand. Lower oil intensity does not reduce vulnerability to the direct damage caused by a disruption in oil supply. Since per capita oil consumption in most developed countries is still several times higher than in developing countries (23 barrels per person per year in the United States compared to 1.5 in China, for instance), developed countries remain highly vulnerable to a disruption in the global oil supply.

.. but they remain vulnerable to higher oil prices

Longer term concerns

Past experience suggests that oil prices are unlikely to remain at the high levels they periodically attain. Nevertheless, the surge in oil prices in 2004 was accompanied by a concern about the possibility of permanently high oil prices in the future, as suggested by the significantly higher prices prevailing in the long-term oil futures markets. This concern is based on a number of arguments concerning both global oil demand and supply.

On the demand side, analysts point to the rapid emergence of China, India and a few other large developing countries that are at an early stage of industrialization or at the beginning of an accelerating phase of demand for energy. For example, China has doubled its oil consumption in the past 10 years and has increased it by more than 10 per cent annually for the past two years. According to some estimates, demand for oil by developing countries will rise from the present level of 25 million barrels per day (bpd) to about 70 million bpd in 2020.

Growth in developing countries will raise the demand for oil ...

On the supply side, there has been a dearth of discoveries of major new oil fields in the past decade or so, as indicated by the deceleration in gross reserve additions. Moreover, some analysts claim that global oil production will probably reach a peak during this decade; some argue that the slowdown in global oil production may have started and that the higher prices in 2004 may be the precursor of a major crisis. In contrast, optimists forecast that new technologies to preserve existing conventional oil reserves will emerge and that the world will begin a transition to the next major sources of energy before mid-century (which is when some forecasts project oil production will peak).

... while the prospects for increased supplies are uncertain

A turning point for the global imbalances?

The global imbalances, particularly the United States twin deficits, continue to raise concerns because of the risks they are widely perceived as presenting to the global economy, not only to the economy of the United States itself. Nevertheless, some observers have argued that the United States current-account deficit poses no such threat because it will be possible to continue financing it over the longer term. The reason given is that such an arrangement is perceived as being mutually beneficial to the United States and to the Asian countries that are now providing a large part of the financing of the deficit by purchasing United States government securities. This arrangement reduces interest rates in the United States below what they would be if other means of financing had to be found and thereby stimulates consumption and investment in the United States, producing higher economic growth and increased imports. For their part, this arrangement allows surplus countries to continue increasing their exports and hence to also achieve higher rates of economic growth.

It has also been argued that the capacity of the United States to borrow abroad has risen because technological advances, continuing global financial deregulation and improvements in transparency and investor protection have created more specialized financial products and institutions. These have increased the ability and willingness of foreigners to place financial resources in the United States and have thereby allowed the United States to finance its current-account deficit without apparent stress. It is therefore claimed that, at least for the United States, there has been an increase in the commonly accepted threshold of around 5 per cent of GDP as the limit for the sustainability of a current-account deficit. These arguments are used to support the view that the current global imbalances could persist for some time without creating difficulties for the world economy. However, the depreciation of the dollar in 2004, particularly in the latter part, suggest that the validity of this argument may be waning.

The impact of the depreciation of the dollar

The explanation for the depreciation of the dollar and its likely effects depends on the conceptual approach that is adopted. One approach focuses on the trade imbalances and argues that the depreciation of the dollar reflects an attempt by the market to restore external balance primarily through its effects on the United States external trade—over time, depreciation is expected to reduce imports and increase exports. There may also be secondary effects, such as an increase in inflation because of higher prices of imports. In addition to a direct dampening effect on domestic demand, increased inflation is also likely to prompt monetary tightening. Monetary tightening will further reduce domestic demand and the demand for imports.

In the case of the United States, these trade effects are likely to be offset by a wealth effect resulting from the large amount of dollar assets held outside the United States. In most countries, the change in relative prices brought about by a depreciation has an expansionary effect on the domestic economy but a contractionary impact on other countries. In addition, however, a depreciation has wealth effects: by reducing its relative wealth, depreciation usually has a contractionary effect within the country. In the case of the United States, the large volume of dollar assets held abroad means that other countries suffer a reduction in wealth (and income from their dollar assets) if the dollar depreciates. This reduction in wealth has a contractionary effect in other countries, compounding the negative wealth effect in the United States itself. This external contractionary effect will adversely affect the demand for United States exports, dampening the effect of the depreciation of the dollar on the trade imbalance.

There are various estimates of the extent of the change in the exchange rate and the decrease in domestic demand required to restore a necessary degree of external balance in the United States, but most evidence suggests that the adjustments required would be considerable because of the nature and magnitude of the United States trade deficit. Since United States imports are considerably greater than its exports, exports have to grow faster than imports even if the trade deficit is to remain unchanged and even faster still in order to reduce the deficit. In 2004, however, the volume of merchandise imports grew faster than exports, despite the prior depreciation of the dollar (which suggests that the J-curve should have begun its positive phase). Imports were driven by the demand for consumer goods, which have an income elasticity of demand greater than that for United States exports. In addition, the United States has become a net importer of capital goods so that the present recovery of investment is also prompting additional import growth. These factors suggest that a depreciation of the dollar alone may not be sufficient to reduce the United States trade imbalance to a sustainable level within a reasonable time.

Depreciation of the dollar alone may not be sufficient to correct its trade imbalance

An alternative approach to analyzing the global imbalances focuses on the fact that the trade imbalances are a mirror image of the differences between savings and investment in individual countries: the external deficit of the United States corresponds to a deficit of its national savings in relation to national investment, whereas countries with current-account surpluses have savings that exceed investment. The gap between savings and investment in a country is, in turn, a reflection of differences in propensities to save, rates of return on investment and related long-term structural factors. These factors give rise to changes in national holdings of international assets which are the counterpart to the current-account imbalances.

The imbalances can also be viewed as differences between national savings and investment

In the case of the United States, there was an increase in the rate of investment with the boom in the technology sector in the late 1990s. This was followed by a fall in investment in 2001 and 2002 with the bursting of the technology bubble and a subsequent recovery in 2003 and 2004. Aggregate savings, however, did not match the increase in investment in the late 1990s, but they have also declined since 2000. A large part of the reason for this decline has been dissaving by the government, primarily as a result of the federal deficit. Following positive public savings (that is to say, a fiscal surplus) as recently as 2000, Government dissaving reached more than 4 per cent of net national product (NNP) in 2004.

The national savings rate in the United States has fallen mostly because of the fiscal deficit

These differences between national savings and investment in the United States were reflected in its financial inflows. In the 1990s, the United States received inflows of FDI and other private capital, notably equity capital, and mostly originating in other developed countries. These inflows were motivated by the higher prospective rates of return in the United States, driven primarily by its faster rate of overall growth and its more rapid technical change. Such private capital inflows were used, directly and indirectly, to finance part of the increase in private investment and thus contributed to the United States technology boom of the late 1990s. The increasing current-account deficit at that time mostly reflected the excess of private investment over private savings in the United States since there was a declining or relatively small fiscal deficit (and eventually a surplus).

In the late 1990s, the deficit reflected a private savings-investment gap ...

With the bursting of the technology bubble in 2001, private capital flows to the United States declined but were increasingly complemented by official flows, particularly purchases of United States government securities by Asian countries with current-account surpluses. These purchases often took the form of direct government intervention in foreign exchange markets in an effort to reduce the appreciation of domestic currencies and thereby maintain the international price competitiveness of exports. The result has been an increase in these countries' foreign exchange reserves (see table I.3), to the extent that reserves now far exceed what used to be considered necessary when reserves were held for precautionary purposes in case of current-account difficulties. With most balance-of-payments problems now originating in the capital account, the optimal level of reserves is less well defined. With the experience of their financial crisis of 1997, Asian countries have reason to be cautious and their present levels of reserves cannot necessarily be deemed excessive. Nevertheless, such reserves yield only a low rate of return and involve the opportunity cost of foregoing a potentially higher return from investment in the domestic economy (or elsewhere).

In sum, the savings of surplus countries were originally being used to secure the higher prospective returns associated with private sector investment in the United States. More recently, these countries' surplus savings have been used in part to finance the burgeoning fiscal deficit and private consumption in the United States. These two phases of financing of the United States external deficits were of global benefit in that they enabled

Table I.3.

Total reserves minus gold: 2000, 2003 and third quarter 2004

Billions of SDRs – end of period			
Country Groups	2000	2003	2004[a]
World	1 556.0	2 123.8	2 425.9
Developed Countries	656.1	820.2	924.5
Japan	272.4	446.4	558.7
Developing Countries	820.0	1 157.2	1 329.6
Africa	61.8	84.1	99.3
Asia	548.2	840.2	982.1
China	129.2	274.7	353.3
Hong Kong SAR[b]	82.5	79.7	80.6
Taiwan Province of China	81.9	139.1	156.6
India	29.1	66.6	78.6
Korea, Republic of	73.8	104.5	118.7
Singapore	61.5	64.4	69.4
Western Asia	89.7	101.2	107.7
Latin America and the Caribbean	120.2	131.7	140.8
Memo items:			
Russian Federation	18.6	49.2	62.2

Source: IMF, International Financial Statistics, January 2005.

a   Third quarter.
b   Special Administrative Region of China.

the United States to fill the role of engine of the world economy for the past several years. In the first instance, foreign private capital contributed to the United States-led global ICT boom of the late 1990s and to the strength of world trade and global economic growth at that time. Subsequently, in replacing private flows, official capital inflows enabled the United States to increase its fiscal deficit during the slowdown and thereby to continue as an engine of global growth and reduce the extent of the slowdown. While this may be rational from an economic or financial point of view, it is the reverse of what might be considered a globally more satisfactory pattern of savings and investment whereby surplus savings in more affluent countries would be used, through various channels, to finance investment in poorer countries.

Restoring balance in the world economy

Notwithstanding their possible prior benefits, the global imbalances may have reached a stage where they pose a potential threat to sustained growth in the world economy because international markets may react in a precipitous or excessive fashion. Similarly, confronted with some of the adverse effects of the imbalances, individual governments may also take actions that could imperil global growth. Of particular concern is the danger of a protectionist backlash because of the competitive pressures emanating from misaligned exchange rates or their uneven correction (as in the case of the euro at present). There could be a reversion to "beggar-my-neighbour" policies in the form of anti-dumping measures and other forms of non-tariff trade barriers. Some domestic constituencies in the United States are already raising concerns about the trade deficit, as reflected in an increasing number of anti-dumping actions against Asian countries and efforts to encourage some of these countries to revalue their currencies. Moreover, "beggar-my-neighbour" policies may extend to non-trade measures, including intervention to manage the exchange rate of floating currencies in order to ensure export competitiveness. In Europe, for example, there are concerns about the degree of appreciation of the euro and its effects on exports and calls for currency market intervention.

> ... but are now increasingly seen as unsustainable

A preferable approach would be to address the imbalances from a global perspective in which the goal should not necessarily be to achieve overall balance in a short period of time. Trade and savings/investment surpluses or deficits may not necessarily be only temporary: long-term imbalances may also be appropriate. Developing countries, for example, would normally be expected to have trade deficits (and corresponding savings deficits) that are financed by inflows of the funds required for their development. For various reasons, some degree of imbalance between developed countries may also be desirable and feasible. In any event, the various structural and institutional differences between the deficit and surplus countries suggest that it is unlikely to be possible to reduce the imbalances to a sustainable level in the short term. A rapid adjustment, such as one that might be adopted by markets if left to their own devices, is likely to be costly so that it should be recognized that the adjustment will be a lengthy process.

> A long-term global approach is required ...

The over-riding need is not to focus directly on correcting the trade imbalances but rather to rebalance the global pattern of growth and of savings and investment. As in all cases of adjustment, attention should not be focused exclusively on the country or region that has a trade or savings deficit because experience suggests that such an approach

> ... in which responsibilities are shared

is likely to be excessively contractionary. Among the surplus countries or regions, all should participate in the adjustment process so that the burden does not fall on one country or region alone.

Higher private sector savings and a reduced deficit are required in the United States

Viewed from this perspective, remedying the imbalances requires not only higher savings in the United States (the deficit country) but also higher investment in the surplus countries, both individually and as a group. In the first instance, there is a need to increase private savings, reduce public dissaving or do some of both in the United States. With the savings of both the public and private sectors having declined in recent years, the preferable solution would be to both encourage private sector savings and reduce the fiscal deficit. Long-term interest rates in the United States already appear likely to increase, both for cyclical reasons and because of the uncertainties associated with the imbalances, and this should stimulate savings in the short run. Additional measures will be necessary to raise the underlying savings rate over the longer term. Federal expenditures are likely to be difficult to reduce in the short run, implying that a reversal of earlier tax cuts should be part of the effort to reduce the fiscal deficit.

Asian surplus countries should channel their excess savings into investment at home or abroad

For their part, countries with external surpluses need to reduce the excess of savings over investment. As those with the largest surpluses, Asian countries should endeavour to restore their investment rates or, if these are already deemed adequate, to channel some of their excess savings to other developing countries where savings fall short of investment needs. Domestically, many of these countries have unmet needs for physical and social infrastructure; they could also invest in measures to improve various forms of social security. Externally, the extensive reconstruction required following the tsunami of December 2004 provides an excellent opportunity for increased investment within the region.

European countries should increase investment aimed at stimulating domestic demand

There is a corresponding need to revitalize investment and growth in Europe. In recent years, the mix of economic policies in most European countries has tended to have the opposite effect, at least in the short term. Attention has been focused on structural reforms, mostly intended to achieve increased international competitiveness and thereby avoid a loss of domestic employment over the longer term. However, the immediate consequences have been negligible increases in real wages and increased doubts about job security. While the former has contributed to strong export growth in some cases, it has dampened domestic demand and inhibited investment and, in some of the major countries, has failed even to achieve its goal of increased employment. The short-term result of these structural adjustments has therefore tended to be contractionary. At the same time, short-term stimulatory actions to counteract these tendencies have been inhibited by the EU rules-based approach to macroeconomic policies. Fiscal expansion has been constrained by the ceilings in the Stability and Growth Pact while the ECB has been bound by its goal of maintaining inflation below 2 per cent. Both the European surplus countries and Japan should use their excess private savings for investment that will shift the balance of growth from the external sector to domestic demand. Alternatively, as with the Asian countries, such resources can be used to improve growth in developing countries.

Implementation would benefit from increased international financial cooperation...

The efforts to reduce the deficits of the United States will have a contractionary effect on the world economy unless complemented and offset by complementary expansionary measures, such as those identified above, in other countries. To ensure that the necessary actions are taken by all concerned in a timely and effective manner, an enhanced degree of international macroeconomic policy coordination is necessary, not only among the major economies but also including the leading economies in Asia.

In order to reduce exchange-rate volatility, these actions should include improved international cooperation in exchange-rate policy. The international community should ultimately strive for a global monetary system that takes into account the interests of all parties when changes in exchange rates are under consideration. Until such a system exists, there should be a cautious approach to changes in exchange-rate regimes because changes in their exchange-rate regimes expose countries to external shocks, with potentially damaging short-term and long-term consequences. As an interim measure, improved cooperation in exchange-rate policy among the major developed countries and with the leading developing economies in Asia should be used to devise a phased and non-disruptive approach to any changes in exchange-rate regimes.

... including in exchange-rate policy

There is already some degree of consensus on the need for macroeconomic measures along the lines identified above but action remains largely lacking because of free rider problems—action by one country may involve costs for the country and yet be largely ineffective unless complemented by actions by others. At present, the inertia of policy makers in addressing the global imbalances is one of the factors causing volatility in international financial markets. As in the 1980s, a clear demonstration of the collective will to tackle the global imbalances would go a long way to reassuring financial markets and increasing the probability that the world economy will be able to maintain growth both over the short term and, while adjustment is taking place, over the medium term.

Collective action is needed to address the macroeconomic imbalances ...

At the same time continued attention needs to be given to the longer-term global development agenda. At the summit meeting of the General Assembly in September 2005, all governments should rededicate themselves to the attainment of the Millennium Development Goals by 2015. This will require concerted efforts by both developed and developing countries. However, as key instruments towards redressing the broader imbalances in the world, attention should be focused on raising the quantity and quality of ODA, improving debt relief for developing countries confronted with unsustainable external debt burdens, and ensuring the equitable and prompt completion of the programme of multilateral trade negotiations agreed at Doha.

... but the long-term development agenda should not be overlooked

Notes

1   See, for example, James D. Hamilton, "What is an oil shock?", *Journal of Econometrics*, vol. 113, Issue 2, April 2003, pp. 363-398; Juncal Cuñado and Fernando Pérez de Gracia, "Do oil price shocks matter? Evidence for some European countries", *Energy Economics*, vol. 25, Issue 2, March 2003, pp. 137-154.

2   See, for example, "Analysis of the impact of higher oil prices on the global economy", International Energy Agency, May 2004, and "The impact of higher prices on the global economy", International Monetary Fund, December 2000.

Chapter II
International trade

International merchandise trade registered a strong performance in 2004, growing at an estimated 10.5 per cent in volume terms, a noticeable acceleration over the 6.2 per cent growth in 2003.[1] This outcome reflected the cyclical strength of the global economic recovery as manufacturing, including the trade-intensive information and communication technologies (ICT) sector, picked up pace in the first half of the year and domestic demand strengthened in a broader number of economies. The brisk global economic environment supported further gains in the prices of commodities and, to a lesser extent, of manufactures, leading to an increase in the dollar value of global trade of almost 19 per cent, to $8.6 trillion, in 2004.[2] However, with the global recovery reaching its peak towards the end of 2004, the rate of growth of global trade is anticipated to moderate to about 8 per cent, in real terms, in 2005 (see table A.7).

> Merchandise trade accelerated in 2004 but some moderation is expected for 2005

In contrast with 2003, much of the trade growth in 2004 originated in developed countries, supported by their faster economic growth, particularly in North America and Japan. These forces were reinforced by the continued strong expansion of the Chinese economy. Import demand of many developing economies also recovered during the year. However, growth and import elasticity differentials among major trading partners and exchange-rate changes, together with past shifts in the location of specific segments of manufacturing, resulted in expanding trade imbalances, which—although not expected to increase further—will persist in the future (see figure II.1).[3]

> Compared with 2003, trade growth was more balanced across regions

Figure II.1.
Selected economies: trade balances, 2003-2005

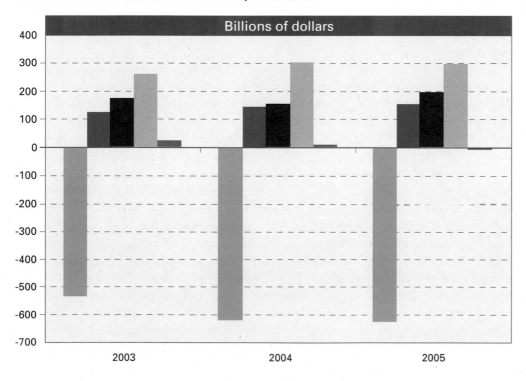

Legend:
- China
- Developing countries excluding China
- European Union
- Japan
- United States

Source:
Project LINK.
Note:
Figures for 2004 are estimates; figures for 2005 are forecast.

The year was also characterized by a continued weakening of the dollar. Nonetheless, for several economies, international demand, particularly from the United States and Asia, was strong enough to offset the negative effects of currency appreciation on exports; this is not likely to be the case in 2005, when import demand is expected to decelerate. China continued to be a formidable presence in international trade, generating about 20 per cent of the observed trade growth and injecting important dynamism not only into intraregional but also to global trade. China's economic growth, particularly the expansion of its manufacturing and construction sectors, has also contributed to an increase in the global demand for raw materials and oil.

Regional trends and outlook

A large trade deficit persisted in the United States but is expected to stabilize

Among the developed economies, there was a lull in the exports of the *United States* around mid-2004, largely due to a slowdown in some Asian economies (China, Japan and Taiwan Province of China and a deceleration in the growth of ICT exports, but data indicate a rebound entering the last quarter, and the annual growth of real exports for 2004 was about 10 per cent, with capital goods taking the lead. Real imports are estimated to have grown at the same pace, driven by an increase in imports of raw materials and capital goods. Real exports are expected to grow by about 10 per cent again in 2005, supported in particular by a weaker dollar exchange rate and strong—albeit moderating—demand from the rest of the world. The growth of real imports is expected to moderate as a result of less vigorous domestic demand. Having deteriorated to about $600 billion in 2004, the United States trade deficit is expected to stabilize at about the same level in 2005 (see figure II.1).

Exports from *Canada* rebounded in 2004 from a decline in volume terms in 2003. The continued adverse impact of the appreciation of the Canadian dollar was offset by increased international demand and higher prices for many of the country's commodity exports. Meanwhile, the acceleration of domestic demand also boosted imports, which will remain strong in 2005. Some moderation in exports is expected in 2005 due to renewed appreciation of the Canadian currency and a slowdown in import demand by the United States.

Export composition had an important impact on export growth in the European Union

In the case of the *European Union* (EU),[4] strong external demand largely offset the decrease in competitiveness stemming from the appreciation of the euro since 2000.[5] Real export growth in the region accelerated and, despite some slowdown during the second half of 2004, is estimated to have reached 6.9 per cent in 2004, compared to 1.5 per cent in 2003 (see table A.7). There was, however, a variety of outcomes within the region. Exports of Germany, for instance, are estimated to have grown by more than 10 per cent. There were also strong performances by Austria, Ireland, Portugal, Spain and most of the new EU members. Conversely, exports by France, Italy and the United Kingdom of Great Britain and Northern Ireland performed poorly. One possible explanation for the German performance is that competitiveness has been bolstered by low increases in unit labour costs compared to the average for the region. Additionally, German exports are particularly geared towards capital goods, which have been a strong component of import demand during the investment rebound phase of the recovery. Among the new EU members, strong export growth in 2004 was due to, among other factors, gains in productivity, which supported competitiveness, and gains in product quality. Moreover, accession to the EU allowed a strong increase in exports of food products, while diversification of export markets continued, particularly towards developing countries.

Import demand accelerated in the EU during the first three quarters of 2004, boosted in part by the appreciation of the euro and an increase in investment spending. With only a moderate pass-through of the currency appreciation into import prices thus far, import demand should remain strong in 2005, bolstered by an improvement in domestic demand. Imports are estimated to have grown 7.4 per cent in 2004, and a similar rate of growth is expected in 2005. Among new European Union members, imports also remained strong, mostly due to the international production chains in their manufacturing. In addition, many companies tried to increase their imports from non-EU countries and accumulate some stocks at the beginning of 2004 since, following accession, such imports became subject to the EU common tariffs. Strong private credit growth also contributed to imports of consumer goods. For these economies, import growth may slow slightly in 2005, in line with exports, but will remain strong due to continuing increases in real wages and an expansion of credit, as well as the implementation of projects associated with EU membership that will require imports of investment goods.

Japan's real export growth has been exceptionally strong for the past two years, reaching 9.4 per cent in 2003 and more than 15 per cent in the first half of 2004, but decelerating in the third quarter of 2004 to an annual rate of 1.5 per cent. Strong demand from the rest of Asia was the key driving force, accounting for more than 90 per cent of the increase in Japan's exports for the past two years, China alone being responsible for more than 40 per cent. The growth of real imports was weaker, but strengthened during 2004, reflecting a recovery of domestic consumption. As a result, the contribution of net exports to GDP turned negative in the third quarter of 2004 for the first time in the past few years. The outlook for Japan's exports has become more cautious for 2005, in line with lower global economic growth and further yen appreciation.

Both *Australia* and *New Zealand* saw growth of imports of over 10 per cent in 2004 owing to their robust domestic demand. Exports also recovered, although both economies are still running a large trade deficit (about 5 per cent of GDP). While Australia—a metal and oil exporter—was able to reduce its deficit owing to improved terms of trade, New Zealand experienced a deterioration in its trade deficit. Trade by both economies is expected to slow: the appreciation of their currencies will weigh on their exports while the anticipated moderation in their domestic demand, particularly in New Zealand, will curb import growth.

The surge in world commodity prices, in particular of oil and gas, and the upturn in the global economy boosted the value of exports of the resource-rich *Commonwealth of Independent States (CIS)* countries. This was supported by buoyant intraregional trade, mirroring the robust growth in the largest economies in the region. Trade is anticipated to slow down in 2005, as exports decelerate due to reduced capacity in the oil sector. Moreover, exports will be constrained by the real exchange-rate appreciation in many countries of the region; this is already reducing the competitiveness of the region's manufacturing, particularly in the Russian Federation. However, exports of manufactured goods remain of limited importance for most CIS countries.

After a strong rebound in 2003, the real export growth of the *Russian Federation* is estimated at about 10 per cent in 2004, led by oil and gas, ferrous and non-ferrous metals and chemicals. Oil exports, however, have been less dynamic than before, largely reflecting uncertainties surrounding a key exporter (Yukos), a new tax system on oil exports and capacity constraints in existing pipelines and terminals. Delays in implementing new pipeline projects will have an adverse effect on oil exports and hence on total

The new EU members experienced strong import growth before accession

CIS countries benefited from increased global demand and higher commodity prices

exports. Meanwhile, robust domestic demand and exchange-rate appreciation led to fast import growth. Terms of trade gains contributed to a widening of the Russian Federation's trade surplus, which reached an estimated $70 billion in 2004.

Developing economies maintained a remarkable trade performance in 2004. *Africa's* exports continued to grow, albeit at a slower pace than in the previous year when there was an impressive recovery in exports in such countries as Madagascar, Nigeria and South Africa. Real export growth was strongest in countries that were able to expand production capacity. New gas and oil fields boosted exports in Algeria and Chad. Similarly, increased output of some mineral commodities accounted for much of the growth in exports by such countries as Namibia and South Africa. Nonetheless, some countries registered a decline in export volumes, mainly because of supply disruptions caused by civil unrest and increased smuggling of key export crops to neighbouring countries. Côte d'Ivoire was a case in point. For the region as a whole, the growth of export volumes is expected to decelerate in 2005 as global demand slows down, while increases in export revenues will be dampened by reduced strength in oil and commodity prices.

Africa increased expenditure on imports in 2004, reflecting an improvement in domestic incomes as well as higher oil and food prices. In many oil-exporting countries, increased investment for the expansion of productive capacities and infrastructure development was the main driving force behind import growth. Meanwhile, adverse weather conditions in the Sahel led to a widening of the cereal deficit and increased imports of food staples in such countries as Burkina Faso, Chad, Mali, Mauritania, Niger and the Sudan.

In *East Asia* merchandise trade expanded by over 18 per cent in real terms in 2004. Merchandise exports have been driven by the positive global economic environment and, at the intraregional level, by strong demand from China. However, some economies in the region (the Republic of Korea, for example) have suffered from their exposure to the volatile ICT and electronics markets, which experienced decelerating growth in the second half of 2004 (see figure II.2) and which are expected to continue to slow in 2005. Others countries (such as Indonesia) have seen their exports come under increasing international competitive pressure. Meanwhile, East Asian merchandise imports have been on an upward trend owing to strong economic growth and higher prices for oil and raw materials. In the case of China and Taiwan Province of China, for example, imports grew faster than exports, leading to a fall in the contribution of net exports to economic growth in these economies.

Looking ahead to 2005, developments in the *China* will continue to be an important determinant of trade performance throughout the region. The predicted modest slow-down of economic growth in China is likely to affect the contribution of net exports to economic growth in economies that are particularly dependent on the Chinese market. In addition, economies such as Singapore are likely to see a dip in their export growth rates due to the impact of the outbreak of SARS in the year 2003 on export growth rates in 2004.

South Asia's external sector reflected the region's healthy economic performance in 2004. The larger countries in the region recorded double-digit growth of both exports and imports, as measured in current dollars. Increases in trade volumes were also substantial, with import volume growth supported by rising domestic investment and consumption demand. Trade is anticipated to continue expanding in 2005, although export growth may slow due to weakening global demand.

As in 2003, India's merchandise trade deficit was offset by strong services exports and remittances, producing a marginally positive current-account balance. In Bangladesh, exports outperformed imports, suggesting that the garment sector finds itself in a position of strength before the end of the Agreement on Textiles and Clothes (ATC)

Increased mining and oil output supported exports by Africa

China has been a key factor in East Asian and global trade performance

Rising domestic consumption and investment led to increased imports in South Asia

Figure II.2.
Semiconductor shipments, January 2000-September 2004

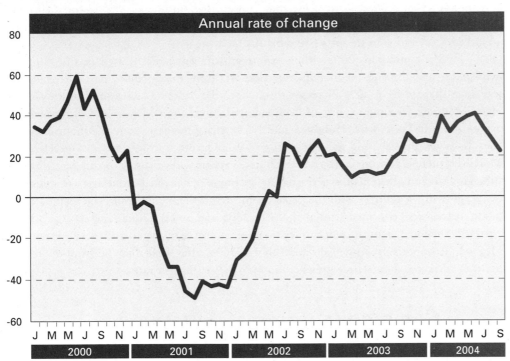

Source:
Semiconductor Industry
Association.

(see section below). Sri Lanka's low water reserves reduced its capacity for hydropower generation and led to higher oil imports for thermal generation, which aggravated the impact of oil prices on the trade balance. High oil prices also weigh on the import bills of the other net fuel importers in the region. Conversely, Iran registered high growth rates in overall exports in 2004 owing to higher oil export volumes and prices. In 2005, Iran's oil export volumes are expected to expand only marginally, owing to flattening production and rising domestic consumption.

  Western Asia's exports grew by 6.7 per cent in 2004. As in 2003, export growth was driven by the oil-exporting countries of the region as oil production increased to meet stronger-than-expected rising world oil demand and also to compensate for supply disruptions in some key producers. Non-fuel exports also expanded in 2004 due to strong performances by Israel, Jordan and Turkey. As a result, the region's total export revenue increased by over 20 per cent in 2004—largely supported by higher fuel prices—but growth is expected to decelerate to 5 per cent in 2005 reflecting reduced oil production and lower prices. Growth of the region's export volume is expected to decelerate to 6 per cent in 2005, with the increase coming mainly from non-oil exporting countries. Meanwhile, import growth accelerated to 7.8 per cent in 2004, reflecting the buoyant economic activity in the region. Consumer goods imports increased, responding to the surge in disposable income in most countries. Imports of capital and intermediate goods also rose owing to increased public and private investments. The lagged expenditure effect of rising government revenues in the oil-exporting countries is expected to support a robust import growth in 2005 as new projects (mostly in infrastructure development, but also in fertilizer, petrochemical and power plants) are planned to be launched during the year.

Higher oil prices
boosted export
revenues in
Western Asia

Latin America
experienced a
balanced trade
performance as
imports recovered

Trade in *Latin America and the Caribbean* gained strength in 2004, as both exports and imports experienced a broad-based recovery. Robust export growth and higher commodity prices supported a second consecutive surplus in the region's current-account balance—an extraordinary event for the region, even more so as it occurred despite a marked acceleration in imports (see table A.7).

In contrast to 2003, when export growth was concentrated in the southern hemisphere and demand for manufactured exports from the northern part of the region was sluggish, exports in 2004 increased throughout the region. The rebound in the United States economy favoured exports of manufactured goods from Mexico and other *maquila* export zones in Guatemala, Honduras and Nicaragua. For these Central American countries, however, this rebound was felt mostly in value terms as export volumes decelerated. Moreover, there is growing concern that Chinese exports will continue to compete with the subregion's manufactures, thus necessitating an improvement in productivity to maintain export growth. In contrast with the situation in the northern subregion, the region's commodity exporters performed strongly both in 2003 and 2004. China's increasing demand especially benefits South American economies, above all, metal and grain exporters. Meanwhile, imports strengthened remarkably in 2004, after weak demand from the region in 2003 when economies were growing, on average, at sluggish rates.

Commodity prices and markets

Non-oil commodities

Continuing the pattern that emerged in 2003, the global economic recovery in 2004 was accompanied by increased prices for many non-oil commodities (see table A.8); following an increase of over 11 per cent in 2003, prices rose by an average of a further 10 per cent in dollars in 2004. The global economic recovery, particularly the rapidly increasing demand in Asia and, within the region, notably in China were the main reasons for the rise in prices in 2004. Overall economic growth in most of these countries is the result of expanding manufacturing activity, for which many of these countries are heavily dependent on imports of commodities. The prospect of continued strong global economic growth, especially the likelihood that manufacturing and investment in China will remain robust, should continue to support commodity prices in 2005.

Despite recent
increases, commodity
prices remain low by
historical standards

The improvement in commodity prices in 2003 and 2004 has not offset the setback suffered in the prior prolonged period of falling commodity prices: from 1980 to 2002, non-oil commodity prices, whether expressed in current United States dollars or special drawing rights (SDRs), fell by some 40 per cent (see figure I.1). Even over the shorter and more recent period prior to the recent upturn, non-oil commodity prices fell by an average of over 30 per cent in dollars and over 20 per cent in terms of SDRs between 1995 and 2002. Particularly for some commodity groups and individual commodities, the improvement in 2003 and 2004 falls far short of returning prices to their earlier levels. At the end of 2004, for example, the price index for all food products was almost 20 per cent below the average for 1995; within this group, the fall in the price of tropical beverages was particularly marked. Developing countries exporting agricultural commodities are therefore still faced with prices that are low by historical standards. Moreover, some of the recent increase in prices has been a reflection of the concurrent depreciation of the dollar; measured in terms of SDRs, the increase in commodity prices since 2002 has been more modest. Finally, the prices of these countries' manufactured imports have continued to increase and, in 2004, were accompanied by higher prices for their oil imports. Even over the past two years, therefore, the terms of trade of some non-oil commodity exporting countries have deteriorated.

Price developments in 2004 differed among commodity groups (a review of recent developments and prospects in individual commodity markets is contained in the annex). In 2003, despite declines for some individual commodities, the average prices for most commodity groups either increased or remained unchanged (see figure II.3). In 2004, increases were more muted and the prices of some commodity groups declined. Reflecting their role as inputs into manufacturing and investment activities, industrial raw materials experienced good demand conditions: prices for minerals, ores and metals rose by an average of more than 20 per cent in 2004. Asian demand has reduced stocks of most metals and these prices are likely to remain high in 2005. Prices for vegetable oilseeds and oils increased because of higher Chinese demand in 2003, but retreated by 10 per cent in 2004. For agricultural raw materials, having risen by more than a quarter in 2003, prices remained largely unchanged over the course of 2004. The prices of food and tropical beverages, the only commodity group which did not experience an increase in prices in 2003, made up some ground and rose by around 8 per cent in 2004, but performance was very mixed within the group. For instance, such commodities as sugar and bananas faced very bullish market conditions, but the prices of wheat, maize and cocoa declined over the year. Excess supply characterizes the markets for several of these commodities; coupled with low income elasticity of demand, even the recent world economic recovery has not led to significant increases in their demand.

Divergent price developments observed across commodity groups in 2004

World oil markets

Oil prices increased and remained extremely volatile throughout 2004. By mid August 2004, prices per barrel were about $14 higher than at the beginning of the year (see figure II.4). The increase was driven by fast growth of demand for oil within a context of low and declining inventories and limited spare capacity, an unsettled security situation that supported a "fear premium" and speculative movements as well as the occurrence of natural disasters that disrupted production in the Gulf of Mexico area. Additionally, world refining capacity proved to be inadequate, while supply from Iraq, as well as from the Russian company, Yukos, remained uncertain.

Oil prices soared amidst strong demand, tight supply and increased uncertainties...

Fears of possible shortages in the world oil market mounted and gained momentum as doubts persisted over the ability of the Organization of the Petroleum Exporting Countries (OPEC) to compensate for any further disruption in oil supplies. OPEC had been producing at more than 95 per cent of capacity, reducing the cartel's spare capacity to only 1 million barrels per day (mbd)—the lowest in three decades—and making oil markets extremely vulnerable to any supply disruption or to a further surge in demand. Even temporary outages in Nigeria and Norway contributed to pressure on prices and reinforced market sentiment that world spare production capacity had been reduced to an alarmingly low level.

Oil prices moderated somewhat after the August peak, only to escalate again in late October 2004 as hurricane Ivan destroyed oil production facilities in the Gulf of Mexico, where 25 per cent of the United States oil is produced and refined. As a result, oil output fell to its lowest level in more than 50 years and stocks of crude oil and refined petroleum products declined in the United States, as opposed to the usual build-up that takes place at that time of the year.

Figure II.3.
Prices of primary commodities and manufactures, January 1999-October 2004
(Indices of US dollar prices, 2000=100)

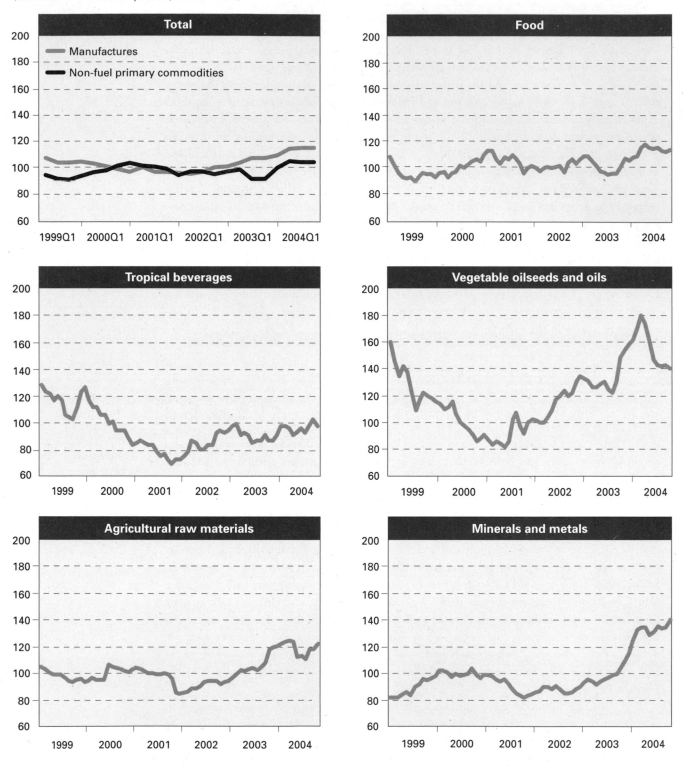

Sources: UN/DESA and UNCTAD, *Monthly Commodity Price Bulletin.*

Figure II.4.
Oil prices and OPEC-10 production quota, January 2003-November 2004

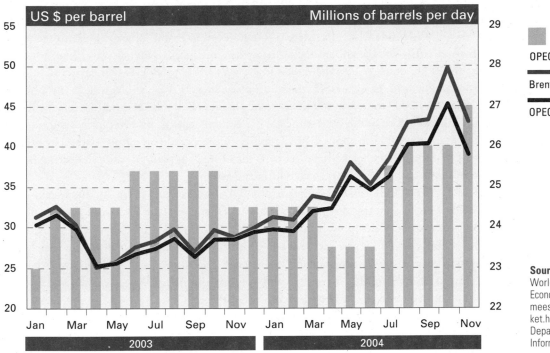

Sources:
World Bank; Middle East Economic Survey (http://www.mees.com/Energy_Tables/basket.htm), United States Department of Energy/Energy Information Agency.

Meanwhile, Iraqi oil output has been struggling to return, on a sustained basis, to pre-invasion levels of about 2.6 mbd, owing to the continued deterioration in the security situation and increased attacks on oil transportation facilities. Oil production fell by 400,000 barrels per day (bpd) to 1.8 mbd in November 2004.[6] Market participants' concerns about a possible prolonged disruption of Iraqi output have been supporting a "fear premium" in oil markets and contributing to the increased prices.

Uncertainties about oil output elsewhere have also enticed speculative funds—mostly hedge funds—into world oil markets. By mid November 2004, however, hedge funds cut their net long positions to the lowest level in a year. At end November 2004, crude oil prices began to weaken (see figure II.4), reflecting mostly the rise in world oil inventories and the anticipation of a relatively mild northern hemisphere winter.

...but moderated towards the end of the year

As prices advanced, OPEC-10 quotas were adjusted upwards (see figure II.4). OPEC-10 production increased sharply during the year, reaching a peak of 28.2 mbd in October 2004—the highest level in 25 years—and above the quota of 26 mbd established for that month. Iraqi production, which is not subject to a quota, added another 2.2 mbd to the Organization's output in October 2004. Most OPEC countries produced above their respective quotas, although the bulk of the increase came from Saudi Arabia and was geared to calm markets and stabilize prices. Increased OPEC production also helped in rebuilding world oil inventories. OPEC production, however, fell in November 2004—the first decline in seven months—mostly due to the drop in Iraqi output and a decline in production by Saudi Arabia.

OPEC output increased in parallel to higher prices...

Amidst concerns about a further slide in prices and higher stock levels in most developed economies, OPEC countries met in Cairo, Egypt, in early December 2004. An additional source of concern for the Organization was the continued dollar depreciation

...and is expected to decline as prices moderate

against major currencies that has been eroding OPEC's purchasing power, as oil prices are denominated in dollars. Accordingly, OPEC member countries decided to keep their production quota unchanged at 27 mbd but committed themselves to eliminate excess supply estimated at 1 mbd (excluding Iraq), effective 1 January 2005.

With Indonesia, the Islamic Republic of Iran and Venezuela exempted from production cuts—as they are producing below their respective quotas—and Iraq not subjected to OPEC quota policy, the remaining seven OPEC producers will carry the bulk of the adjustment, with Saudi Arabia contributing the most. OPEC also agreed to meet by the end of January 2005 to review and assess trends in global oil markets and to decide whether further cuts would be needed. After the OPEC announcement, however, prices fell, reflecting the market skepticism about OPEC's ability to keep crude oil output within its official limit of 27 mbd. Nonetheless, the forecast is for OPEC supply to decline, reflecting mainly output cuts and better compliance within the group.

Output by non-OPEC countries also increased and will continue to expand in 2005

Non-OPEC output increased by 1.1 mbd to 50.1 mbd in 2004, less than expected. This was mostly due to the impact of Hurricane Ivan and weak growth of the Norwegian output. Oil supply from non-OPEC countries is projected to rise in 2005 as output in the Gulf of Mexico recovers and production in Canada expands. Increased production in Azerbaijan, Kazakhstan and the Russian Federation, as well as in Latin America and the Caribbean (Brazil and Trinidad and Tobago) and Africa (Angola, Chad and Sudan) will also contribute to the projected increase in 2005.

Robust economic growth led to increased oil demand

Despite some slowdown in the second quarter of 2004 (see figure II.5), world oil demand increased by 3.3 per cent to 81.8 mbd in 2004, the fastest rate of growth and the largest absolute increase since 1977. Vigorous economic growth in China was the driving force behind the strength of global oil demand. Robust growth in the United States, as

Figure II.5.
World oil supply and demand, first quarter 2003-third quarter 2004

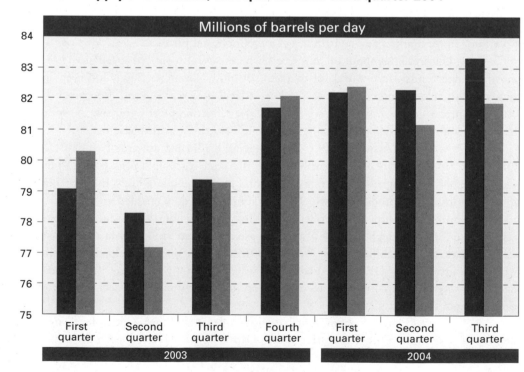

Supply

Demand

Source:
International Energy Agency,
Monthly Oil Market Report.

well as in India and other Asian economies, contributed to the increased demand. Global oil demand is expected to continue to increase in 2005, albeit at a decelerating rate, that is to say, by 1.5 mbd to 83.3 mbd, compared to 2.6 mbd in 2004. Low growth in world oil demand in 2005 reflects mostly the expected deceleration in economic growth in such major oil consumers as China and the United States.

As in the past two years, the global oil market will remain tight in 2005. Equally important for price developments is the "fear premium". As long as the security situation continues to deteriorate in Iraq and threats to oil and installation facilities persist in Saudi Arabia and elsewhere, the "fear premium" will remain high. However, the anticipated deceleration of demand, together with some compliance slippages by OPEC and increased production elsewhere, is expected to push prices down in 2005. As a result, average Brent oil prices are forecast to be around $38 pb (per barrel) in 2005, lower than the average of $40 pb recorded in 2004.

Lower oil prices are forecast for 2005

Trade policy developments

Doha negotiations: the adoption of a framework agreement

With the adoption of the framework agreement of 1 August 2004 (the "July package"),[7] the World Trade organization (WTO) negotiations under the Doha Work Programme resumed. The momentum generated by the adoption of the agreement must be sustained in the coming months if the agreed frameworks are to be translated into detailed and specific modalities for concluding negotiations, taking account of the development objectives of the Doha Declaration.

The "July package" sets out frameworks for future negotiations in five core areas: agriculture, market access on non-agricultural products, services, development issues and trade facilitation. It also recognizes that the original deadline of January 2005 for completion of the Doha round was unrealistic. It is now expected that negotiations will continue after the Sixth Ministerial Conference of the World Trade Organization to be held from 13-18 December 2005 in Hong Kong Special Administrative Region (SAR) of China.

Frameworks for negotiations on five areas were launched

The framework agreement has three key process-related aspects. First, participants had agreed to resume work in all negotiating bodies in February-March 2004, with the aim of agreement on specific negotiating frameworks and modalities in core negotiating areas by the end of July 2004, thus putting the Doha negotiations back on track. These meetings, the first since the WTO Cancún Ministerial Meeting, were seen as a cautious and gradual process to rebuild consensus and mutual confidence. Second, recognition emerged that the process and substance of negotiations were inseparable and that agenda-setting was critical in determining the outcomes of negotiations. Third, the July agreement owed much to a qualitative improvement in the overall negotiating atmosphere. Thus, increased attention has been given to direct and informal contacts among WTO Members, and there has been greater disposition to listen to the positions and concerns of others, especially in such crucial areas as agriculture.

During these negotiations, developing countries keenly pursued their interests and priorities, demonstrating enhanced negotiating capabilities and strengthened regional, interregional, and issue-based coalitions. These strengthened coalitions (G-20, G-33, G-90, etc.) have been successful in focusing the negotiations on the core trade agenda and in

Increased relevance of country coalitions in the negotiations

advancing their specific development concerns. Equally significant have been some North-South coalitions (such as the G-10 and the Cairns Group) and negotiating "ginger groups", such as the Five Interested Parties (FIP) (Australia, Brazil, the EU, India and the United States), which came together to São Paulo on the eve of the Eleventh United Nations Conference on Trade and Development (UNCTAD XI) and prepared much of the ground for the framework agreement on agriculture.

Main areas of the framework agreement

Agriculture. The framework agreement on agriculture[8] is the most important result of the Doha process so far. It expresses a commitment to reduce substantially production-linked farm supports and eliminate agricultural export subsidies. Nonetheless, the exact timetable, in terms of the base periods, commencement, duration and completion of implementation, are left open.

The clear commitment to eliminate all forms of *agricultural export subsidies* "by the end date to be agreed" has been regarded as "historic". In addition to existing subsidies, the framework aims to set up a modality to eliminate other export competition measures, such as trade-distorting types of export credits, guarantee and insurance programmes and export subsidy elements in the programmes of state-trading enterprises. Furthermore, rules are to be developed to ensure that food aid does not displace commercial trade, and the negotiations will also consider whether all food aid could be provided in grant form. Under the agreement, developing countries would be allowed to maintain certain export subsidies to market and transport their products "for a reasonable time", even after other export subsidies are eliminated.

With regard to *domestic support measures*, the WTO's Agreement on Agriculture (AoA) classifies such measures into three types, the so-called boxes:

- The amber box comprises measures considered to distort production and trade (with some exceptions), including support price measures and subsidies directly linked to production quantities; amber box support is subject to certain limits.
- The blue box comprises support measures that require some kind of reduction of production such as acreage, number of animals, etc. (there are currently no limits to blue box subsidies).
- The green box comprises activities with no trade or at least minimally trade-distorting support, often not targeted at a particular product and not linked to price support or production. These subsidies do not face any limit.

Although the AoA tends to differentiate between trade-distorting and non- or minimally trade-distorting measures, it can be argued that in a world characterized by imperfect financial markets and where farmers are faced with credit constraints, any subsidies—by providing additional finance—allow recipient farmers to increase output relative to a situation where subsidies would be unavailable.

Trade-distorting subsidies to be reduced but details still to be negotiated

The July framework maintains the subsidy differentiation mentioned above and aims at substantially reducing trade-distorting subsidies to domestic production, including capping the blue box support,[9] with a "tiered approach" (that is to say, involving several different levels of reduction). It will require countries with the highest subsidy levels to make the deepest cuts. As an initial installment, it is envisaged that the total level of trade-distorting domestic support, as bound under the Uruguay Round commitments, be cut by at least 20 per cent in the first year of implementation. The framework also aims to reduce the circumvention of the reduction commitments (for example, through switching support between products), which was possible under the structure of the Aggregate Measurement of Support (AMS). In order to take account of the special development role of agriculture, developing countries will not be required to cut certain domestic supports provided to subsistence and resource-poor farmers.

In the *market access pillar*, "substantial overall tariff reductions" are to be achieved, with high tariffs subject to the biggest cuts. However, under the concept of "sensitive products", developed countries can maintain a high level of tariff protection on specific products provided that they expand the tariff rate quotas on these products and that they compensate for this with greater liberalization for other products. Developing countries would make lesser tariff reductions, as a form of special and differential treatment, and would have the right to designate "Special Products" and to apply a "Special Safeguard Mechanism" for food security and rural development purposes. Despite the strong appeal from developing countries, however, the framework agreement does not foresee any provisions regarding non-tariff barriers and market entry conditions. (The incidence of non-tariff barriers has been increasingly felt as tariffs are lowered.) It is agreed that LDCs would be exempt from any reduction commitment, and their concern about guaranteeing duty- and quota-free market access would be addressed in the negotiations.

> Tariff protection to remain high for "sensitive products"

Special and differential treatment (SDT) was recognized as an integral part of all elements of future agricultural negotiations. It would be particularly crucial as regards the market access pillar. Commitments by developed countries to reduce domestic support substantially and to eliminate export subsidies are seen as serving to correct the long-standing imbalance in the AoA. Therefore, SDT could to a large extent be seen as an issue for the market access pillar in terms of both increased market access for developing countries and ensured flexibility to protect their sensitive sectors and Special Products.

The framework agreement also stipulated that *cotton* would be dealt with as part of the agriculture negotiations, but that it would be "addressed ambitiously, expeditiously and specifically" under a new sub-committee. The negotiations are to encompass all trade-distorting policies affecting the sector, from import tariffs, trade-distorting domestic support subsidies and export subsidization. The new sub-committee on cotton was established and started its work in November 2004.

> Cotton subsidies will not be treated as a separate track

Market access for non-agricultural products (NAMA).[10] Participants agreed on the "initial elements" of modalities for future negotiations. The aims remain ambitious, but the specifics of key elements, such as the tariff reduction formula, the special terms for developing countries and the issue of preference erosion, are to be negotiated later.

The main initial elements that would form the basis for negotiations for a reduction of tariffs are as follows:

> The basic elements for NAMA negotiations were established

- An ambitious formula to cut tariffs: a non-linear approach to be applied on a line-by-line basis, with deeper cuts for higher tariffs for all products, without *a priori* exclusions. Some developing countries are concerned that a non-linear approach could require them to make deeper tariff cuts than the developed countries, contrary to the provision of the Doha Ministerial Declaration for less than full reciprocity. The text also foresees possibilities for more ambitious tariff cuts (or elimination) for certain sectors (so-called sectoral initiatives), including those of interest to developing countries.

- Credit for autonomous liberalization by developing countries, but only for those measures taken since the end of the Uruguay Round (1994). This in effect excludes the most substantial liberalization by many developing countries.
- Special treatment of developing countries: developing countries would have longer transition periods and flexibilities in tariff cuts.
- Exemption of LDCs from tariff reductions. LDCs would be required only to substantially increase the level of their tariff bindings in order to enhance transparency and trade predictability. Developed countries and "other participants who so decide" are invited to provide LDCs with duty-free and quota-free market access to support diversification, develop supply capacities and increase their integration into the multilateral trading system.
- Provision of general guidelines for addressing the issue of non-tariff barriers to trade through notification, identification, examination, categorization and ultimate negotiations.

New deadline for revised service offers was set

Services. The framework on services negotiations largely reiterates the previous objectives for this segment of negotiations, while emphasizing the need to ensure the high quality of offers. Revised offers are to be made by May 2005, although it is uncertain whether all developing countries or LDCs would be in a position to make new or revised offers by then. Although services did not attract much attention in the July framework negotiations, it remains a core agenda item under the Doha Work Programme. As of 1 November 2004, 44 out of 147 WTO Members had made initial offers, of which 29 were developing countries. Most developing countries are still identifying their specific offers, the barriers to their services exports, the impact of requests by developed countries on their services sectors, as well as means to overcome supply constraints through implementation of Articles IV and XIX of the General Agreement on Trade in Services (GATS), which call for efforts to increase the participation of developing countries in international trade in services. Progress needs to be made on the assessment of trade in services, which remains an integral part of the negotiations on services.

Few improvements offered by developed countries on their Mode 4 market access commitments

Participants also agreed to pursue services trade liberalization in sectors and modes of supply of export interest to developing countries. So far, however, among the initial offers submitted, some major developed countries have made no improvements in their market access commitments for Mode 4 (temporary movement of natural persons). The new offers continue to relate to measures regulating commercial presence rather than measures regulating other areas. Furthermore, developing countries are seeking to prevent a protectionist backlash on information technology (IT)-enabled services trade. Locking in the current liberal regimes regulating this type of trade would ensure that the interests of developing countries were reflected in the negotiations. The July package also reconfirms that there would be no *a priori* exclusions of any services from the negotiations. This implies that developing countries will be able to pursue their interests in, for example, construction and maritime services, sectors where limited offers have been made so far.

Limited advances made on the most contentious issues

A balanced outcome in negotiations would also depend on progress in GATS rule-making, where negotiations on Emergency Safeguard Measures (ESM) remain one of the most contentious areas. Developing countries have emphasized the need for the disciplines on ESM to address the implications of liberalization. Little progress has been achieved in the discussions under Article XV of the GATS concerning the need for and possible scope of disciplines on subsidies in services. Article XIII of the GATS provides for negotiations on government procurement of services, but these have not yet produced any concrete results. In addition, negotiations concerning disciplines on domestic regulation have also produced few results so far.

Development issues. The Framework agreement reiterates calls for the strengthening of WTO provisions on special and differential treatment (SDT) in favour of developing countries and implementation issues. It instructs the Committee on Trade and Development in Special Session to complete the review of all categories of SDT provisions with clear recommendations for a decision by July 2005. On implementation issues, the General Council should review progress and "take any appropriate action" no later than July 2005 on the basis of the report of the Director-General of the WTO, to be submitted no later than May 2005. These deadlines seek to avoid the previous pattern of work on development issues since the launch of the Doha negotiations, characterized by missed deadlines and minimal progress.

In addition, it was agreed that special attention should be given to the specific trade-and-development-related needs and concerns of developing countries, including capacity constraints. In this context, the trade-related issues associated with the fuller integration of small, vulnerable economies into the multilateral trading system are also to be addressed, without creating a subcategory of members, as part of the Doha Work Programme.

The WTO General Council decision also affirmed that developing countries and low-income countries in transition, and in particular LDCs, are to be provided with enhanced trade-related technical assistance and capacity-building to increase their effective participation in the negotiations, to facilitate their implementation of WTO rules and to enable them to adjust and diversify their economies. In this context, the General Council welcomed and further encouraged the improved coordination with other agencies, including under the Integrated Framework for Trade-related Technical Assistance for the Least Developed Countries (IF) and the Joint Integrated Technical Assistance Programme (JITAP).

> Developing countries, in particular LDCs, are to be provided with enhanced technical assistance

"Singapore" issues. Negotiations on trade facilitation (improving the movement, release and clearance of goods, including goods in transit) were officially launched. Developing countries were reassured they will not be required to take on commitments they cannot implement, (such as, for financial reasons) and were promised substantial support and assistance in implementing future commitments. Moreover, it was recognized that the extent to which LDCs and developing countries could enter into commitments, and the timing with which they did so, would depend on their implementation capacities, and implementation would not be required where they lacked the necessary capacity. The other Singapore issues—trade and investment, trade and competition policy, and transparency in government procurement—were dropped from the negotiating agenda. At the first meeting of the Negotiating Group on Trade Facilitation held on 15 November 2004, WTO members agreed on a Work Plan and a schedule of meetings.

Bilateral and regional trade arrangements burgeon

The number of bilateral regional free trade agreements (RTAs) continued to rise in 2004. The forging of RTAs over the last decade appears to have gained pace in the wake of the impasse at Cancún on the Doha negotiations. Between January and August 2004, 21 RTAs were notified to the WTO, increasing the total number of notified preferential agreements in force to 206. In addition, around 30 agreements were signed between 2003 and 2004 and are awaiting entry into force, and approximately 60 RTAs are in the negotiations/proposal stage. The intensification of RTA activities has been recorded across all regions, but it has been more pronounced in the Latin America and Caribbean and in the Asia-Pacific regions (see box II.1).

Box II.1

Multilateralism, free trade agreements in Asia and the Pacific: progress, challenges and prospects

The Asia-Pacific region provides important evidence of the complementarity between open trade and investment policies and regionalism. There are more than 50 regional trade agreements (RTA) involving Asia-Pacific economies, of which 48 have been notified to WTO. These RTAs vary considerably in membership, style, design and effectiveness, in line with the diverse and heterogeneous nature of the political and economic landscape of the Asia-Pacific region. In the region, RTAs may involve free trade agreements (FTAs) in which duties and other restrictive regulations on commerce are eliminated substantially on the trade among participating countries; or some type of preferential trade agreement (PTA) between countries. Some RTAs have well-developed, institutionalized rules of interaction, while others have a more informal structure based on voluntary cooperation. Some are open to new members; others have placed a moratorium on new members. The breadth of coverage varies as well, with services covered in a few agreements while most do not cover services in any meaningful way. Agriculture may be wholly or partially excluded, while movement of factors of production, depth of tariff cuts, coverage of non-tariff measures and decision-making processes vary widely. Likewise, the results achieved vary greatly.

A variant of the many trade agreements signed over the past few years is bilateral trade agreements that go beyond border measures, extending into wide-ranging areas of domestic policy-making. They thus encompass a deeper integration of trade through the harmonization of a wide range of trade practices, procedures and standards.

Despite the recent rapid growth of RTAs, including their bilateral format, it is not clear in which direction regionalism is moving. Broadly, two major trends can be distinguished. First, there is a trend directed at coalescing existing regional groupings into outward-oriented FTAs that bridge sub-regions and continents. This holds the potential to lay the foundation for the eventual integration of all countries of the region into a forward-looking Asia-Pacific zone of efficient production, with enhanced opportunities for world trade. The locus of this integration is centred around East and South-East Asia. Progress in bringing about the China-ASEAN FTA has been faster than initially expected, notwithstanding a missed deadline of 30 June 2004. With a market of nearly 1.8 billion people, a regional gross domestic product (GDP) of about US$ 2 trillion, international trade worth US$ 1.2 trillion and current average annual economic growth of 8 per cent, this will become an important production base and trade and investment centre of the region. The addition of Japan, which has long worked at strengthening its economic ties with the members of ASEAN, is further boosting the integration process.

Box II.1 (cont'd)

A second trend can also be distinguished. Instead of amalgamating RTAs into wider bridging initiatives, there is a splintering into bilateral FTAs. For example, the United States Framework Agreement under the Enterprise for ASEAN Initiative in effect consists of a series of bilateral FTAs with individual ASEAN countries. The United States-Singapore FTA is the first to have been concluded, to be followed by similar agreements with Australia, the Philippines and Thailand, and others in the pipeline. Similarly, Japan has indicated that it has concerns about the varying levels of industrial development between the founding and newer members of ASEAN and prefers to enter into a series of bilateral trade agreements with individual member countries of ASEAN. It has also started with Singapore, to be followed by the Philippines, Thailand and others in the pipeline. China is also negotiating separate bilateral agreements with a number of ASEAN countries, including India and Pakistan.

Both proactive and defensive trade strategies seem to be driving the processes in the Asia-Pacific region. On the one hand, major trading powers appear to be competing to establish trade predominance in the region; on the other hand, there are a number of smaller trading countries that are equally active in forging bilateral trading arrangements and also appear to be competing to establish dominance as a hub. This, however, may be more symptomatic of a defensive trade strategy, designed to avoid finding themselves at the spoke end of another major hub. A multi-layered constellation is thus emerging, made up of a dominant hub-and-spoke arrangements with substrata of other hub-and-spoke arrangements in which smaller economies are trying to establish alternative hubs. The option of developing countries collectively establishing themselves as the alternative hub, through ASEAN, stands out.

These conflicting trends are indicative of tensions in the evolution of the international trade architecture. Their successful resolution is fundamental to ensuring that the multilateral trading system be strengthened, that it operates more efficiently and that it work for the benefit of all countries and their peoples.

More than one third of global trade now takes place between countries that have some form of reciprocal RTA. As agreements proliferate, a single country often becomes a member of several different agreements. For example, the average African country belongs to four different agreements and the average Latin American country belongs to seven. This creates a "spaghetti bowl" of overlapping arrangements, each with different rules of origin, tariff schedules and periods of implementation, all complicating customs administration.

An increasing share of global trade takes place between RTA signatory countries

The most notable developments in the latest phase of RTA proliferation include the expansion in the number of cross-regional RTAs, of developed-developing country RTAs and the emergence of agreements among developing countries. Negotiations on RTA multilateral rules (in the Negotiating Group on Rules) launched at Doha to clarify and improve the relevant disciplines and procedures under existing WTO provisions may help to resolve the current impasse in the WTO Committee on Regional Trade Agreements (CRTA) regarding compliance with WTO rules. So far, these negotiations have made progress only on transparency issues. The resumption of negotiations in 2004 has advanced the Group's work on transparency to the point where one of the procedural improvements considered by the Group (to ask the Secretariat to prepare factual presentations of RTAs under examination) has been forwarded to the CRTA for testing, on a preliminary and voluntary basis. The Group has also enlarged the scope of its negotiations to include systemic issues, which may suggest increasing concern by Members about the possible effects of RTAs on third parties and on the multilateral trading system as a whole.

Negotiations were launched to clarify compliance of RTAs with WTO rules

Implications of ATC Termination

Textiles and clothing trade governed by the Agreement on Textiles and Clothing (ATC), and earlier by the Multifibre Arrangement (MFA) and its predecessor arrangements, represented a derogation from the basic principles of the multilateral trading system for more than 40 years (see table II.1). The integration of the textile and clothing sector into the main WTO rules at the end of 2004 is therefore expected to contribute to the "upholding and safeguarding of an open, non-discriminatory, predictable, rule-based, and equitable multilateral trading system." While countries will be affected differently, on the whole, the elimination of restraints in the sector should also contribute to the realization of the United Nations Millennium Development Goals.[11]

Table II.1.
The history of international trade in textiles and clothing

Date	Action taken
1957: January	Five-year agreement reached with Japan on limiting overall textile exports to United States.
1958: November	United Kingdom signs "voluntary" limitation on cotton T&C products with Hong Kong after threatening imposition at lower than prevailing volume levels.
1959: September	United Kingdom signs similar restraint agreements with India and Pakistan.
1960: November	GATT Contracting Parties recognize the problem of "market disruption", even if it is just threatened; serves as "excuse" for establishing future non-tariff barriers (NTBs).
1961: July	The Short Term Arrangement (STA) is agreed upon.
1962: February	The Long Term Arrangement (LTA) is agreed upon to commence on 1 October 1962 and last for five years.
1966: June	The United Kingdom implements a global quota scheme in violation of the LTA. (The LTA provides only for product-specific restraints.)
1967: April	Agreement is reached to extend the LTA for three years.
1969-71	The United States negotiates voluntary export restraints (VERs) with Asian suppliers on wool and man-made fibers.
1970: October	Agreement is reached to extend the LTA for three years. (It was later extended an additional three months to fill the gap until the MFA came into effect.)
1973: December	It is agreed that the MFA will begin on January 1, 1974, and last for four years.
1977: July	The European Economic Community and the United States negotiate bilateral agreements with developing countries prior to agreeing to extension of the MFA.
1977: December	The MFA is extended for four years.
1981: December	The MFA is renewed for five years. The United States, under pressure from increased imports resulting from dollar appreciation, negotiates tough quotas.
1986: July	The MFA is extended for five years, to conclude with the Uruguay Round.
1991: July	The MFA is extended pending the outcome of the Uruguay Round negotiations.
1993: December	The Uruguay Round (UR) draft final act provides for a 10-year phase-out of all MFA and other quotas on textiles in the ATC. The MFA is extended until the UR comes into force.
1995: 1 January	1st ATC tranche liberalized by importing countries – 16% of 1990 import volume.
1998: 1 January	2nd ATC tranche liberalized by importing countries – 17% of 1990 import volume.
2002: 1 January	3rd ATC tranche liberalized by importing countries – 18% of 1990 import volume.
2005: 1 January	4th ATC tranche liberalized by importing countries – 49% of 1990 import volume.

Source: Based on D. Spinanger, "Faking Liberalization and Finagling Protectionism: The ATC at Its Best", Table 1. Background Paper for the WTO 2000 Negotiations: Mediterranean Interests and Perspectives, Cairo, 14-15 July 1999.

By late 2004, only 51 per cent of the products covered under the ATC had been integrated. Many textiles and clothing items of particular interest to developing countries were still restricted, and the commercial significance of the integration for these countries had been very limited. This results from the fact that the integration programme was left to the discretion of the restricting countries, which opted to defer integration of the majority of restrained products until the last moment, back-loading integration of about 80 per cent of their restrained textiles and clothing goods until the final two-year phase of the integration programme. However, in 2004, restraining countries formally notified the WTO of their intention to meet commitments to eliminate all remaining quota restrictions as scheduled under the ATC.

Considerable delays occurred, thus restricting many products of interest to developing countries

The termination of the ATC is an important development that should strengthen the multilateral trading system, and many developing countries are expected to increase their exports of textiles and clothing significantly. However, LDCs and small economies that enjoyed quota- and duty-free treatment of their exports to the United States and the EU (through the African Growth and Opportunity Act (AGOA), "Everything But Arms" (EBA) and Generalized System of Preferences (GSP) initiatives), and that rely heavily on exports of assembled garments, seem vulnerable to the expected increase in competition in the sector following the expiry of the ATC. For many of them, textiles and clothing are extremely important sources of foreign exchange earnings; for example, in Asian LDCs like Bangladesh, Cambodia, the Lao People's Democratic Republic and Nepal, the sector earns 50 to 90 per cent of the countries' international trade revenues. Exports in this sector are also important for many African countries, especially for cotton-producing countries in West Africa (Benin, Burkina Faso and Mali), while clothing exports are significant for Kenya, Lesotho, Madagascar and Mauritius. While adjustment may be mitigated by the fact that trade in the textiles and clothing sector is growing by some 6 per cent a year, some studies indicate that preference-receiving countries could be adversely impacted by the elimination of quotas. These countries also have limited capabilities to adjust to the impacts of preference erosion that will accompany ATC expiry and may need international support to adapt to the more competitive situation in the sector.

Some developing countries enjoying trade preferences may be vulnerable to the ATC termination

Another important concern for developing countries is that the liberalization of textile and clothing trade on the basis of normal WTO rules and disciplines may lead to the replacement of quotas with contingency protection measures like anti-dumping actions and special safeguard contingency protection measures. The restraining countries have initiated numerous cases since the ATC took effect. For example, the EU alone initiated 53 anti-dumping cases in the textiles and clothing sector between 1994 and 2001[12] and the United States invoked 28 special safeguard measures under the ATC by October 2001.[13] These contingency measures were used for imports under quota restrictions and were targeted towards individual enterprises, often small and medium-sized ones, which do not have adequate resources to defend their cases.

There is concern ATC termination may trigger other sorts of protective measures...

The potentially damaging effects of anti-dumping actions are of particular concern in the post-ATC era. Many of the anti-dumping filings could be termed "process filers" that significantly hinder foreign exports during the investigation stage. For example, one study found that anti-dumping duties on average have caused the value of imports to contract by 30 to 50 per cent.[14] Moreover, the potential threat of an anti-dumping action could force a firm to sell the product in question at a much higher price than it would under normal circumstances. An exporting firm's pricing behaviour to avoid an anti-dumping duty could result in sub-optimal use of its competitive advantage. Against this background, the member countries of the International Textiles and Clothing Bureau (ITCB)

...of which anti-duping actions are particularly worrisome

have proposed to the WTO that developed Members adopt a grace period of two years after the expiry of the ATC during which they do not initiate investigations into imports of textile and clothing products from developing countries.[15] This proposal was based on the Doha Ministerial Declaration and the Decision on Implementation-Related Issues and Concerns.[16] Most recently, concerns have been also expressed regarding a possible revival of voluntary export restraints (VERs), a concept which is prohibited by WTO rules and disciplines. Against this background, in December 2004, China announced that it would impose taxes to restrict the exports of certain textile products; this was widely viewed as a pre-emptive measure against further anti-dumping and other safeguard measures by major importing countries. By potentially increasing the prices of such products, the measures may delay the removal of distortions in the textile and garment market, thus limiting the gains consumers could receive with the expiration of the ATC. With little information available on the lines of products to be taxed and the tax rate to be applied, however, it is not clear what impact these measures will have. Competitors claim that, due to Chinese efficiency and low labour costs, the measures may have only a limited restraining impact. Manufacturers of higher-end products, in turn, are concerned that the measures may encourage Chinese producers to shift production to higher value-added, upscale products, which would pose intensified competition.

Notes

1. Unless otherwise specified, trade figures refer to the average of exports and imports. Growth rates refer to volume terms while values refer to current United States dollars. Finally, figures refer to merchandise trade only.

2. In contrast with 2003, average commodity prices recorded gains in Special Drawing Rights (SDRs) comparable to those measured in dollar terms.

3. See chapter I for an analysis on global imbalances.

4. Data and analysis on the trade of the European Union includes intra-EU trade.

5. During 2001-2004, the euro appreciated by more than 50 per cent against the dollar; in trade-weighted terms, the appreciation was over 30 per cent.

6. International Energy Agency, *Oil Market Report*, Paris, 10 December 2004.

7. Decision on the Doha Work Programme, adopted by the General Council of the World Trade Organization on 1 August 2004, document WT/L/579.

8. World Trade Organization document WT/L/579, annex A.

9. Support under production-limiting programmes.

10. See, World Trade Organization document WT/L/579, annex B.

11. For more details, see *Assuring Development Gains from the International Trading System and Trade Negotiations: Implications of ATC Termination on 31 December 2004*, note by the UNCTAD secretariat, document TD/B/51/CRP.1.

12. World Trade Organization, "Anti Dumping Actions in the Area of Textiles and Clothing: Developing Members' Experiences and Concerns", TN/RL/W/48/Rev.1, 5 February 2003, p. 2.

13. World Trade Organization document G/C/W/325, op. cit., p. 14.

14. T. J. Prusa, "On the Spread and Impact of Antidumping", Working Paper 7404, NBER Working Paper Series, 1999.

15. World Trade Organization document WT/GC/W/502.

16. The former agreed to improve disciplines under the Agreements on Implementation of Article VI of the GATT 1994, and the latter calls for the examination of Article 15 of the Anti-Dumping Agreement relating to special and differential treatment of developing countries with a view to operationalizing it as a mandatory provision.

Annex:
Developments in non-oil commodity markets

Agricultural commodities

Among tropical beverages, *coffee* provides a good illustration of the dualism of trends in tropical soft commodities. While the composite price index for coffee increased by some 29 per cent during the first 11 months of 2004, price trends were markedly divergent across different types of coffee. For example, the average price of Arabica coffees rose by 8 per cent while Robusta coffee prices decreased by roughly 10 per cent during the same period. This situation largely reflects market fundamentals in leading producing countries, as output of arabica in Brazil decreased sharply, while robusta output in Viet Nam experienced strong growth. As a result, total exports of arabica fell by 2 per cent in 2003/04 compared to 2002/03, whereas exports of robusta increased by 1.8 per cent over the same period. Despite efforts by the international community to increase the demand for coffee, the growth of world coffee consumption remains only around 2 per cent a year. However, the decision by the United States, the world's largest coffee consumer, to rejoin the International Coffee Organization (ICO) after a 10-year absence may contribute to strengthening ICO activities to boost demand. Nonetheless, the currently high level of stocks may still temper any sustainable bullish development in coffee markets in the near future.

Cocoa prices decreased by 2 per cent in 2004 (see table A.8). As in the case of coffee, market fundamentals were the main driving force. World cocoa production reached a new peak in 2002/03 and is anticipated to have increased further in 2003/04. Ghanaian output expanded by 46 per cent in 2002/03 and increased by an estimated further 20 per cent in 2003/04. The surge in Ghanaian output was largely due to a national campaign to apply fertilizer and spray against black pod, as well as the effect of the increase in prices during the 2002/03 crop harvest. Similarly, higher farm prices in Côte d'Ivoire contributed to supply increases in that country.[a] Despite a sizeable expansion in grinding capacities in Asia (two new cocoa processing factories were established in Malaysia) the world cocoa market has returned to surplus and this is weighing heavily on price developments. World cocoa bean stocks went up by 100,000 tonnes in 2002/03 and are anticipated to increase by 40,000 tonnes in 2003/04. With the resurgence of conflict in Côte d'Ivoire in November 2004, however, concerns about supply disruptions re-emerged,[b] and are expected to boost international cocoa prices in early 2005.

With the exception of a peak in September 2004, the price of *tea* remained flat during the period January to November 2004. Expectations of lower production by some leading producers did not materialize and global tea output in 2004 is estimated to have been at its 2003 level, around 3.1 million tonnes. Nonetheless, a slight recovery in prices might be expected in the near future due to the revitalization of consumption in the Middle East and in the CIS countries and to the fact that Iran and the Libyan Arab Jamahiriya lifted their bans on Indian tea imports.

The price of *sugar* increased by over 34 per cent from December 2003 to November 2004, more than offsetting the decline observed at the beginning of the year. Prices are expected to remain strong in the near future as the 2004/05 harvest is forecast to suffer a shortfall of 2.8 million tonnes due to adverse weather conditions in India[c] and China. However, the potential for growth in sugar production in Brazil and the high level of world sugar stocks might curb favourable price development in the long run.

Wheat and maize prices suffered a downturn during the course of 2004, after a favourable year in 2003 (see table A.8). The Food and Agriculture Organization of the United Nations (FAO) estimated world cereal output at 1,985 million tonnes in 2004—some 5 per cent higher than in 2003—as European producers recovered from the drought of the previous year. Persistent downward pressure on prices of cereals might be expected in view of the rebound in world production and stagnant world demand. Maize for feed and industrial usage is an exception to this trend as demand is still likely to grow significantly.[d]

Conversely, the price of *rice* rose sharply during 2004 and is likely to be strong in the near future. World trade of rice, however, is expected to have decreased by 6 per cent in 2004, largely owing to reduced imports by some Asian and South American economies that benefited from an increase in their own domestic production. World rice output is forecast to grow by 4 per cent in 2004/05. The world production increase, however, is not going to be enough to meet global demand, which could reach a record level of 413 metric tons (MT) in 2004/05. Stocks are therefore expected to fall again and prices to remain strong.

After a sharp decrease in 2003, *banana* prices went up by nearly 34 per cent during the first 11 months of 2004. This upturn was largely due to supply-side problems, including poor weather conditions and labour strikes in banana-producing countries. For instance, Colombian exports were often delayed and the fruit deteriorated as a result. A consultation between the EU and Latin American and Caribbean producers on the future tariff on imports of bananas started at the beginning of October 2004. This forms part of the EU reform of the banana regime, which will change from the present tariff and quota system to a tariff-only system from 2006. This will affect banana prices in the long run.

Among *vegetable oilseeds and oils*, the prices of cotton oilseeds, soybean oil, palm oil and groundnut oils fell in 2004, while prices of palm kernel oil, coconut oil and sunflower oil increased. As in the case of coffee, price developments in this commodity group are driven mainly by market fundamentals. World trade in vegetable oils has been slowing because of a deceleration in demand. Prices of vegetable oilseeds and oils are expected to fall further as total world stocks are increasingly high, having expanded by 53 per cent in 2004/2005.

Although **cotton's** competitiveness vis-à-vis polyester fibres improves as oil prices increase, the outlook for the price of cotton is not favourable. A decrease of about 35 per cent in both Cotton Outlook Indexes A and B was observed during the year. Prices may fall further as good weather and the use of new technologies are leading to increases in output in most producing countries, with peak harvests expected in Brazil, China, India, Pakistan and the United States. According to the International Cotton Advisory Committee (ICAC), world cotton supply is anticipated to rise by 17 per cent in 2004/05,[e] marking the largest annual increase in world supply since 1984/85. Although consumption is likely to increase by roughly 3 per cent in the same period, world cotton supply will exceed consumption and stocks are expected to increase substantially.

Despite the bullish pattern between March and July 2004, due to higher oil prices, the price of *natural rubber* remained flat in 2004. Prices, however, stayed relatively high, benefiting suppliers from the three leading producing countries (Indonesia, Malaysia and Thailand), while demand was driven mainly by China, which now accounts for 20 per cent of world consumption. With a possible softening of oil prices, however, natural rubber may lose its competitiveness in the near future as it coexists with a range of synthetic rubbers derived from petroleum products.

Minerals and metals

Minerals and metals prices have been on an upward trend since late 2002, particularly when measured in dollars. Continued strong economic growth in China and improved economic prospects in the rest of the world kept the boom in metals alive in 2004. Prices had already reached high levels for those metals (such as nickel) for which supply conditions were tight at the early stages of the accelerating phase of the current global business cycle. Others, such as aluminium and copper, saw rapidly falling stocks at a later stage and experienced stronger price increases in 2004.

Metal prices appeared to have reached a peak in early 2004, when the prices of several metals fell. In some cases, this was a response to the announcement by the Government of China of measures to rein in economic growth. Yet, after a few months of weaker prices, the upward trend resumed, with prices of most metals reaching new peaks in October 2004 before retreating. Speculative interest contributed to the strength of prices (see box) and concerns about speculative bubbles have been voiced. The end-year declines, however, do not seem to indicate the beginning of lower prices for metals, but rather corrections by market participants liquidating large holdings. Without exception, demand is outpacing supply of non-ferrous metals.

The outlook for 2005 depends on the magnitude of the expected slowdown in China's economic growth and the extent to which this will be offset by rising demand in other parts of the world. Overall, with stocks low and demand expected to increase, albeit at a slower rate, the prices of metals are likely to maintain the levels of 2004.

The production of *aluminium* was about 3.6 per cent higher in the period January to September 2004 than in the same period in 2003 and industry inventories remained virtually unchanged.[f] London Metal Exchange (LME) stocks, however, fell by more than 700,000 tons, or by about 3 per cent of annual production, indicating an emerging imbalance between supply and demand. Prices of alumina, the raw material for

Box

Impact of speculation on short-term commodity price developments

Bullish commodity prices tend to attract financial investors who, in turn, are likely to exert an influence on price developments in commodity markets. In the present global environment, any decision to transfer financial investments from stock markets to small commodity futures exchanges tends to intensify the upward trend in the prices of most commodities. According to the Swiss Futures and Options Association, hedge funds are currently pouring billions of dollars into commodities markets. For instance, on the New York Mercantile Exchange (NYMEX), futures and options volumes in the first three quarters of 2004 were 20 per cent and 25 per cent respectively larger than in the first three quarters of 2003, a year that shattered long-standing records. On the soft commodity side, increasing volatility in the cocoa market, sharpened by the crisis in Côte d'Ivoire, is also boosting the volumes of futures and options traded on both the London International Financial Futures and Options Exchange (Liffe) and New York Board of Trade (NYBOT) exchange. This is partly the result of a return to risk management strategies by producers and consumers. However, the fact that commodity prices and the prices of equity and bonds often move in opposite directions tends to attract speculative interest during periods of financial turmoil and low returns in equity markets.

aluminium, have remained at historically very high levels, and were pushed even higher in the later months of the year because of hurricane damage to refineries and ports in the Gulf of Mexico and Jamaica. Aluminium prices increased by some 17 per cent during the first 11 months of 2004. Measures adopted by China to curb production in some energy-intensive industries as well as energy shortages in that country during 2004 also helped to support higher prices. If production growth in China slows significantly in 2005, inventories will decline more quickly and prices may remain at the present level or even increase.

The *copper* market has experienced three years of widening supply deficits which have resulted in a drawdown of stocks and rising prices. In the first eight months of 2004, copper usage rose by 5.9 per cent compared to the same period in 2003, while refined production increased by 2.7 per cent, mainly as a result of strong growth in the production of secondary copper. The addition of refining capacity in 2005 and 2006 will lead to lower prices, but probably not before 2006, owing to the need to build up badly depleted industry stocks.

The demand for *iron ore* continued to expand rapidly in 2004. In spite of a 10.7 per cent increase in production in the first half of the year compared to the same period in 2003, signs of shortage emerged as smaller steel producers were forced to suspend operations due to lack of raw materials. *Steel* prices were high throughout the first ten months of the year, again spurred by rapidly expanding demand, mainly in China but also in other regions. The rapid expansion of China's steel production, which resulted in China becoming a net exporter of steel in September 2004, did not appear sufficient to meet the growth in global demand. Since world steel production is expected to continue to grow at historically high rates, iron ore prices will likely repeat their 2004 performance in 2005 and increase by some 18 per cent or more.

Lead prices rose rapidly in 2004. China, the world's largest producer, continued to absorb a growing part of its own production. In the rest of the world, production fell despite increased reliance on recycling, and a supply deficit emerged. The addition of new mining capacity in 2005 will result in a smaller deficit, which may lead to prices falling from their high levels of late 2004.

The *nickel* market has experienced a long period of supply deficit, mainly due to the very rapid growth in demand for stainless steel in China. Although volatile, prices have stayed at very high levels. In 2004, the demand and supply gap appears to have shrunk owing to greater use of stainless steel scrap and of other types of stainless steel containing less nickel. Nevertheless, since no new major source of primary nickel is expected to enter operation before 2006, there is little prospect of the supply deficit being significantly reduced in the short-to-medium term. A small supply deficit is expected to persist in the longer term (until 2011), even if all currently planned additions to capacity are implemented. It is therefore unlikely that the price of nickel will fall significantly in the medium term.

Tin prices have risen rapidly as a result of strong demand, particularly in China. Supply was unable to keep up with demand, especially after the closure of the Renison mine in Australia in 2003.[g] LME stocks have fallen to a level corresponding to less than two weeks of world usage. Demand is likely to continue to grow rapidly, particularly since lead in solder is being replaced by tin for environmental reasons (for instance, the EU is to ban the use of lead in various electronic devices in 2006[h]). Tin prices are therefore expected to remain at historically high levels.

The prices of *zinc* also rose in 2004 as signs of a supply deficit became clearer. The International Lead and Zinc Study Group forecasts a deficit of 150,000 tonnes in 2004, shrinking to 100,000 tonnes in 2005, after which production is expected to increase substantially.[i] However, despite some decrease, LME stocks were still high at slightly less than 700,000 tonnes in November 2004, providing an ample reserve supply. While the supply-demand balance indicates a continued strengthening, price rises are expected to be modest.

Notes

a   "The high farmer (sic) price in Côte d'Ivoire during the 2002/03 harvest clearly had a beneficial impact on levels of husbandry and fertiliser input which gave a significant boost to output in 2003/04" (ED&Fman Cocoa Market Report, November 17, 2004).

b   In addition to supply disruptions, delays in selling cocoa beans might have an impact on the quality. As a result of the conflict, a large number of producers decided to store the cocoa in inadequate conditions, running the risk of quality deterioration. According to Radio France International, at the end of November 2004, cocoa exports in Côte d'Ivoire declined by 70,000 tonnes compared to the same period in 2003.

c   "Sugar production in India is forecast to fall dramatically by 51per cent from the previous year to 13.8 million tonnes" (FAO, *Food Outlook,* Rome, September 2004).

d   According to the FAO, "food consumption of cereals is likely to grow at a much lower pace with food use of wheat and rice staying below their long term trend" (FAO, *Food Outlook,* Rome, September 2004).

e   Press release of the International Cotton Advisory Committee, November 2004.

f   See www.world-aluminium.org

g   The Renison mine was scheduled to reopen in November 2004 (*Metal Bulletin,* London, 6 September 2004).

h   "Time for tin", *Mining Journal,* London, 27 August, 2004.

i   Forecasts quoted in "China to become net importer of zinc—ILZSG", *Metal Bulletin,* London, 18 October 2004.

Chapter III
Financial flows to developing and transition economies

The net private financial flows of $59.6 billion received by developing countries in 2004 represented a decline from 2003, but were still substantially higher than the average level recorded for 1998-2002 (see table III.1). Total net flows from all sources also fell from 2003 levels, basically because of scheduled repayments under multilateral financial institution lending programmes. Foreign direct investment (FDI) remained the largest source of net private financial inflows in 2004 and began to recover from the depressed levels of recent years. Net financial flows to countries with economies in transition turned negative in 2004 owing to sharply lower net private financial flows to the Russian Federation.

Net private financing declined in 2004

Table III.1.
Net financial flows to developing countries and economies in transition, 1993-2004

Billions of dollars				
	1993-1997	1998-2002	2003	2004[a]
Developing countries				
Net private capital flows	152.7	36.6	64.5	59.6
Net direct investment	88.0	141.8	129.9	141.4
Net portfolio investment[b]	69.0	-12.8	-10.4	-18.1
Other net investment[c]	-4.2	-92.3	-55.0	-63.6
Net official flows	11.9	10.6	-18.6	-27.4
Total net flows	164.7	47.1	45.9	32.2
Change in reserves	-78.5	-94.9	-323.8	-312.8
Economies in transition				
Net private capital flows	8.4	1.2	25.9	-9.3
Net direct investment	4.4	7.6	8.5	11.5
Net portfolio investment[b]	-0.2	-3.3	-3.6	-8.2
Other net investment[c]	4.1	-3.2	21.0	-12.7
Net official flows	7.2	-0.2	-4.3	-1.6
Total net flows	15.6	1.0	21.7	-10.9
Change in reserves	-4.7	-9.0	-37.0	-30.1

Source:
International Monetary Fund (IMF), *World Economic Outlook Database*, September 2004.

a   Preliminary.
b   Including portfolio debt and equity investment.
c   Including short-and long-term bank lending, and possibly including some official official flows to data limitations.

Net transfer of financial resources increases

Reverse net resource
transfers continue
to increase

As a result of low net financial flows and large foreign exchange reserve accumulation by developing countries, net outward financial transfers[1] from developing countries continued to increase in 2004 (see table III.2). This means that for the seventh straight year, developing countries as a group have transferred resources to developed countries. Net transfers from East and South Asia moderated, but remained at a high level. As a result of continued external surpluses, countries in the region continued to accumulate large holdings of foreign exchange reserves, mainly low-risk securities of developed countries. Exchange intervention in order to stabilize currencies with respect to the dollar has added to these accumulations. While the majority of these increasing reserves continue to be invested in United States securities, there has been evidence over the year of Asian central banks and oil-exporting countries increasing the diversification of their reserve holdings to include more euro-denominated securities. Nonetheless, the increase in dollar holdings in 2004 continued to be an important source of financing for the current-account deficit of the United States.

Net financial transfers from Latin America increased in 2004, mirroring the improved trade and current-account surpluses for the region as a whole. In contrast with the recent past, this result was largely due to robust export growth relative to strengthening of import growth. The financial outflows were used to make debt repayments, but there was also an increase in official reserves for precautionary purposes.

Table III.2.

Net transfer of financial resources to developing economies and economies in transition, 1995-2004

	1995	1996	1997	1998	1999	2000	2001	2002	2003	2004[a]
	Billions of dollars									
Developing economies	52.2	29.9	3.6	-35.0	-112.0	-167.5	-142.4	-196.4	-268.5	-312.7
Africa	6.4	-5.2	-2.7	16.0	6.2	-24.4	-12.2	-4.6	-19.3	-33.3
Sub-Saharan (excluding Nigeria and South Africa)	7.6	5.6	7.6	12.3	9.3	3.0	8.2	5.4	6.0	2.7
East and South Asia	25.9	23.6	-29.6	-130.2	-134.1	-109.1	-108.9	-140.2	-151.6	-138.2
Western Asia	20.5	9.8	11.0	32.7	3.9	-34.1	-26.4	-20.2	-40.0	-74.3
Latin America	-0.7	1.7	24.8	46.5	12.0	0.0	5.2	-31.4	-57.6	-66.9
Economies in transition	-3.4	-7.0	3.2	1.6	-25.3	-49.3	-30.1	-26.6	-35.4	-35.4
Memorandum item: Heavily indebted poor countries (HIPCs)	7.0	6.6	7.0	9.8	10.2	6.2	7.4	7.2	7.2	8.5

Source:

UN/DESA, based on International Monetary Fund (IMF), *World Economic Outlook, September 2004,* and IMF, *Balance of Payments Statistics.*

a   Preliminary estimate.

Private financial flows:
reduced risk premia, but limited flows

International financial markets in 2004 were dominated by the expectation of rising interest rates in the United States as the Federal Reserve responded to the recovery of growth in the economy with a return to a more neutral monetary policy. Accompanied by a reduced appetite for risk by international investors, uncertainty in the first half of the year over the size and timing of the new policy was reflected in a rise in United States long-term interest rates that translated into a widening of the spread between yields on emerging market bonds and that on the risk-free benchmark United States treasury securities at the beginning of the second quarter of 2004 (see fig. III.1). After the Federal Reserve made it clear that the upward adjustment in policy rates would be "measured", expectations of a rapid adjustment in United States interest rate expectations moderated and increased the attractiveness of higher yields on emerging market securities. As a result, investor sentiment began to improve and yield spreads began to narrow after the Federal Reserve announced in late June the first of what would by year's end be five consecutive increases of 25 basis points in the federal funds rate and the discount rate. This improvement in sentiment was reinforced by the United States bond market's interpretation of the rising short-term policy rates as insuring future price stability and led to a decline in United States long rates, increasing the attractiveness of emerging market investments. Although this resulted in a reversal of the widening of yield spreads on bonds of emerging markets, the episode underscores the vulnerability of these spreads, particularly in the case of emerging market bonds with low credit ratings, to the prospect of further increases in international interest rates.

Changes in US monetary policy set the tone in international financial markets

Figure III.1.
**Yield spreads on emerging market bonds,
1 January 2003-30 November 2004**

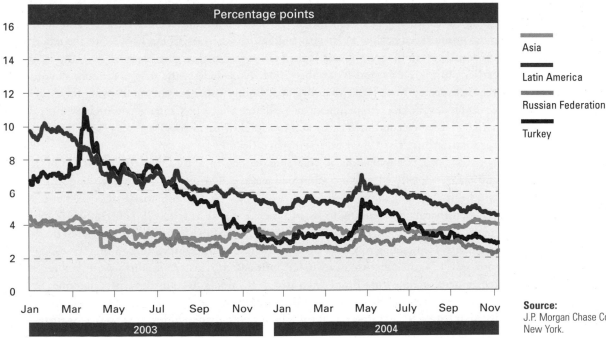

Source:
J.P. Morgan Chase Co.,
New York.

**Financial markets
adapt to higher
US interest rate**

The continued improvement in stability in emerging financial markets is in part due to the deleveraging of international speculative positions that has occurred over the past several years, as well as to strengthened export growth that has continued to increase the capacity of these economies to service external debt. Higher levels of international reserves, greater use of flexible exchange rates and active debt management operations by some large emerging markets, such as Brazil and Mexico, also contributed to reducing vulnerability. In addition, continued progress in the implementation of adjustment policies after the earlier financial turmoil in Brazil and Turkey enhanced investor confidence. Consequently, the credit rating of the sovereign debt of emerging markets improved during the year and was a factor in the orderly adjustment of these markets to the rise in international interest rates in 2004.

**Access to international
financial markets
improves for emerging
market issuers**

Emerging markets have benefited from this improved sentiment through strong net issuance of bonds in international and local currency markets in 2004, supplementing a high level of issuance in the first quarter with a substantial rebound in the second half of the year. Many countries, including those with relatively low creditworthiness, were able to take advantage of favourable conditions in international markets early in 2004 and in the second half of the year to fully fund their financing needs for 2004 and to pre-fund some 2005 needs. A number of local currency bond markets, including in Brazil and Turkey, also received increased international investment early in the year. As a result, the market disruption in April and May had little effect on the ability of emerging markets to fund their needs for the year. Additionally, sovereign and corporate borrowers from Latin America and Turkey were able to access the market again in June. Net issuance by Asian countries declined substantially for the year, reflecting reduced borrowing by China, Indonesia and Thailand. Net bond issuance by economies in transition remained strong in 2004, with the majority accounted for by Russian natural resource corporations and an increase in sovereign bond issuance by the Czech Republic.

**Emerging market
equity markets follow
the trend in the US**

Equity prices in emerging markets were also affected by difficulties early in the second quarter and declined across the board in tandem with the temporary sell-off in developed country stock markets. International investment flows to stock markets in developing countries dropped substantially in the second quarter of 2004 as a result, with the most pronounced decline in Eastern and Southeastern Asian markets. With the rebound in stock markets in the second half of the year, prices in emerging markets generally recovered earlier peak levels by mid-November 2004. Nonetheless, the net investment flow for the year is expected to be lower than in 2003. Equity issuance remained strong for the year as a whole, despite the retrenchment in April and May, but China accounted for most of the activity. Issuance continued to be at a low level in Latin America as a whole, but Brazilian corporations increased their borrowing significantly.

**Bank lending remains
subdued as
international banks
adjust risk exposures**

Net bank lending to emerging markets in 2004 followed the pattern of decline and recovery observed in bond and stock markets. During the decline, lending to East and Southeast Asia was the most resilient, while new bank credit to Western Asia and Africa declined sharply and lending to Latin America was at a standstill. Net lending to developing countries in 2004 remained unchanged from 2003, with Asian countries the largest recipients. Net lending to China slowed however, as official measures to limit credit demand took effect. Latin America as a whole continued to register net outflows in lending as net repayments, mainly from Brazil, increased. Net lending to countries with economies in transition is estimated to have declined moderately from 2003 owing to decreased borrowing by Russian banks. This region remained reliant on net bank lending as a source of financing.

Foreign direct investment recovers

Global FDI inflows rose by 6 per cent in 2004 to $612 billion (see table III.3), ending the downturn that started in 2001. The increase was the result of a 48 per cent increase in flows (to an historic high of $255 billion) to developing countries and Central and Eastern Europe,[2] which more than offset the fourth consecutive year of decline (from $380 billion in 2003 to $321 billion in 2004) in flows to developed countries. FDI inflows remained unevenly distributed and concentrated in a few key destination countries.

The expectation of a consolidation of the global economic recovery, rising equity market valuations and an increase in mergers and acquisitions (M&As) augur well for global FDI flows in 2005. Both developed and developing countries are expected to attract an increase in flows, although the traditional recipients will continue to dominate inflows, indicating a return to the norm following the situation in 2003-2004. The United States, the United Kingdom of Great Britain and Northern Ireland and a few large European economies will receive higher flows and China and India are both expected to achieve record inflows, as well as serving as major contributors to the growing FDI flows to developing economies. The global stock of FDI is expected to increase to over $7 trillion, embodying the activities of some 61,000 transnational corporations (TNCs) with over 90,000 foreign affiliates.

The continued decline in FDI inflows to developed countries was due to large repayments of intra-company loans for some host countries, notably Belgium, Germany[3] and the Netherlands. Luxembourg and Spain, both major recipients of FDI in 2003, received lower inflows in 2004. However, FDI inflows to the United Kingdom and the United States, two of the largest host countries, recovered from a dip in 2003, partially because of increased M&A activities and an improved intracompany loans position.

All developing regions saw an increase in FDI inflows in 2004. Inflows to *Africa* rose for the second consecutive year, to $20 billion. Enhanced investor perceptions and changes in regulatory framework contributed to this performance. The high prices of key commodities encouraged transnational corporations (TNCs) to pursue new exploration projects in African countries, and a large part of the increase in FDI came from investment in natural resource exploitation, driven by the demand for diamonds, gold, oil, platinum and palladium. Such natural-resource rich countries as Algeria, Angola, the Libyan Arab Jamahiriya, Mauritania, Nigeria and South Africa received more FDI than in 2003. Flows to the Libyan Arab Jamahiriya increased because of the end of sanctions in 2003. The prospects for flows to such countries in 2005 are similarly favourable. In addition, the extension of the African Growth and Opportunity Act (AGOA) of the United States to 2015 should reinforce the positive trend by encouraging the expansion of production of all types of products for export to the United States in Africa.

Asia and the Pacific received more than $166 billion in FDI inflows in 2004, a 46 per cent increase over 2003. The key factors behind this growth were improved economic performance, changes in FDI policy, improved corporate profitability, a rise in M&A activities in the region and, particularly between North-East Asia and South-East Asia, further regional integration, which encourages production networks and intraregional FDI flows. All subregions witnessed increases in flows compared to 2003. China, Hong Kong Special Administrative Region (SAR) of China, India, the Republic of Korea and Singapore saw markedly higher inflows, with the result that flows to the region remained unevenly distributed and dominated by a few economies. Mainly due to higher flows to

Growth of global FDI resumes

The outlook for FDI inflows in 2005 is positive

Inflows to developing countries increase in 2004

A major increase in FDI inflows goes to Asia and Pacific

Table III.3.
Foreign direct investment inflows, by host region and major host economy, 2001-2004

Billions of dollars				
Host region/economy	2001	2002[a]	2003[a]	2004[b]
World	818	681	580	612
Developed countries	571	490	380	321
European Union	357	374	308	165
Belgium	..	15	29	7
France	50	49	47	35
Germany	21	36	13	-49
Ireland	10	24	27	26
Italy	15	15	16	15
Luxembourg	..	117	92	52
Portugal	6	2	1	6
Spain	28	36	26	6
United Kingdom	53	28	21	55
Australia	4	14	8	5
Canada	27	21	7	12
Japan	6	9	6	7
United States	159	63	30	121
Developing economies	220	159	173	255
Africa	20	12	15	20
Latin America and the Caribbean	88	53	51	69
Brazil	22	17	10	16
Chile	4	2	3	6
Mexico	27	15	11	18
Asia and the Pacific	112	94	107	166
China	47	53	54	62
Hong Kong SAR[c]	24	10	14	33
India	3	3	4	6
Korea, Republic of	4	3	4	9
Singapore	15	6	11	21
Central and Eastern Europe[d]	26	31	27	36
Czech Republic	6	8	3	5
Poland	6	4	4	5
Russian Federation	2	3	7	10

Source:
UNCTAD (www.unctad.org/fdistatistics) and UNCTAD's own estimates.

Note:
World FDI inflows are projected on the basis of 101 economies for which data are available for part of 2004, as of 29 December 2004. Data for most economies are estimated by annualizing their three quarterly data. The proportion of inflows to these economies in total inflows to their respective region or sub-region in 2003 is used to extrapolate the 2004 data for Africa, Asia and the Pacific and Central and Eastern Europe. For 2004, Latin America and the Caribbean is estimated by annualizing the three quarterly data for principal host economies and by the 2003 data for the economies for which no data are available so far.

a Revised data.
b Preliminary estimates. See note above.
c Special Administrative Region of China
d The eight countries that acceded to the EU in 2004 are included in this region.

China and the Republic of Korea, North-East Asia continued to dominate flows to the region, followed by the ASEAN (Association of Southeast Asian Nations) and South Asia subregions. Singapore was the largest recipient of FDI within ASEAN, while India occupied this position in the South Asia subregion. Flows to the Central Asia and Western Asia subregions rose as a result of higher investment in the oil sector. Flows to the Pacific subregion increased only marginally. A further improvement in economic conditions and further opening to FDI in the region will enhance prospects for 2005.

FDI flows to *Latin America and the Caribbean* increased in 2004 for the first time in five years, by 37 per cent to $69 billion. Improvements in the economic situation and changes in the policy environment were the main factors behind the rebound. Brazil and Mexico accounted for half the inflows to the region in 2004. While there was a recovery in flows to Mexico, inflows to Brazil were largely unchanged. Flows to Chile rose and those to Argentina recovered marginally. The improving economic situation and efforts to streamline investment procedures should further improve the prospects for FDI flows to the region in 2005 and beyond.

FDI flows to Central and Eastern Europe rebounded in 2004, reaching a record high of $36 billion, following $27 billion in 2003. The surge in flows involved three quarters of the countries in the region. The eight new member countries of the European Union (EU)—the group mostly affected by the downturn in 2003—experienced the largest increases. Led by Romania and Bulgaria, flows to Southern and Eastern Europe also grew rapidly. FDI flows to the Russian Federation rose to close to $10 billion. Prospects for FDI flows to the region in 2005 remain bright.

The continuing opening to FDI contributed to the strong flows of FDI in 2004. In 2003, there were 244 changes in laws and regulations affecting FDI, 220 of which were in the direction of more liberalization (see figure III.2). In that year, 86 bilateral

Inflows to Latin America and the Caribbean are positive for the first time in five years

Domestic environment for FDI inflows improves

Figure III.2.
Bilateral investment treaties and double taxation treaties concluded, cumulative and year to year, 1990-2003

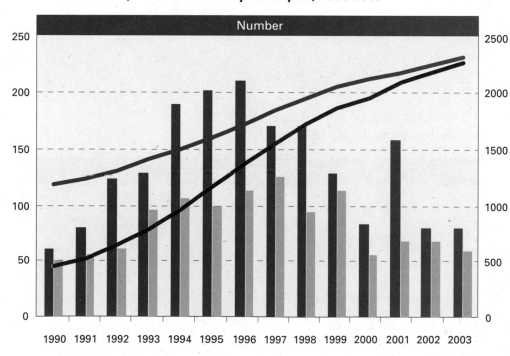

BITs (total per year: left axis)

DTTs (total per year: left axis)

Total BITs (cumulative: right axis)

Total DTTs (cumulative: right axis)

Source:
UNCTAD, BIT/DTT database
(www. unctad.org/fdistatistics).

investment treaties (BITs) and 60 double taxation treaties (DTTs) were concluded, bringing the totals to 2,265 and 2,316, respectively. However, the annual number of new treaties concluded has been declining, since 2002 in the case of BITs and since 2000 in the case of DTTs. This decline could partly be attributed to the increase in the number of bilateral and regional FTAs, most of which include provisions on investment, usually covering investment liberalization, facilitation, promotion and protection. More bilateral and regional FTAs were also initiated and negotiated in 2004.

Patterns of FDI flows are changing

The global pattern of FDI flows has been changing as countries increasingly compete for FDI by adopting less restrictive national policies. Economies with strong growth and more liberal regulatory frameworks have attracted larger flows. In both developed and developing countries, there has been an increase in FDI in services, partly because of the increasing tradability of services and partly because of the drive by firms to improve their cost competitiveness. A third change is the increasing amount and share of the global stock of FDI accounted for by developing countries.

Developing countries are also a source of FDI

Developing countries have assumed a growing role as a source of FDI, as reflected in the fact that the share of developing economies and Central and Eastern Europe in the global stock of outward FDI rose from 7 per cent in 1990 to 11 per cent in 2003 (see table III.4). However, these outflows were concentrated among a few countries— only 15 economies accounted for 92 per cent of the total stock of outward FDI from developing regions in 2003 (see table III.5). The Asian economies were the fastest growing investors, with China and India emerging as the most notable (see figure III.3).

The growing competitiveness of developing country enterprises and their desire to obtain access to markets, resources, technology and strategic assets have been the key reasons for the growth in their outward FDI. Encouragement from their governments through incentives, bank loans and a relaxation in their policies towards outward FDI has helped. The relocation of production activities to lower cost locations and the growth in intra- and interregional FDI flows also encouraged outward FDI flows from developing countries.

Table III.4.
Stock of outward foreign direct investment, by country groups of origin, 1990 and 2003

Billions of dollars		
	1990	2003
World	1 758.2	8 196.9
Developed countries	1 629.0	7 272.3
Developing countries	128.6	858.7
Central and Eastern Europe	0.6	65.9
Share of developing countries and Central and Eastern Europe in world total (percentage)	7.3	11.3

Source:
UNCTAD, FDI/TNC database
(www.unctad.org/fdistatistics).

Table III.5.
Developing economies and territories with largest stock of outward foreign direct investment, 1990 and 2003

Millions of dollars		
Country	1990	2003
Hong Kong SAR[a]	11 920	336 098
Singapore	7 808	90 910
Taiwan Province of China	12 888	65 232
Brazil	41 044	54 646
China	2 489	37 006
Korea, Republic of	2 301	34 531
Malaysia	2 671	29 686
British Virgin Islands	..	26 810
South Africa	15 027	24 195
Cayman Islands	694	21 884
Argentina	6 105	21 303
Mexico	1 070	13 815
Chile	178	13 784
Panama	4 188	8 742
Venezuela	2 239	7 950

Source:
UNCTAD, FDI/TNC database
(www.unctad.org/fdistatistics).

a Special Administrative Region of China.

Figure III.3.
Outflows of foreign direct investment from China and India, 1990-2003

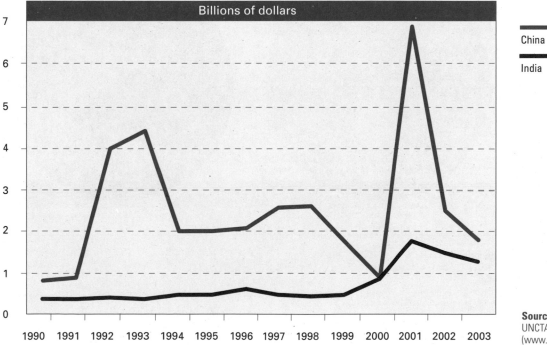

Source:
UNCTAD, FDI/TNC database
(www. unctad.org/fdistatistics).

Growth of FDI in services[4]

A significant development regarding global FDI flows has been the shift towards services. Services accounted for some $500 billion, about two thirds, of total FDI inflows during 2001-2002. In the early 1970s, services accounted for only one quarter of the world FDI stock; in 1990, this share was less than one half but, by 2002, it had risen to almost 70 per cent, or an estimated $4 trillion (see figure III.4). Over the same period, the share of the primary sector in the world stock of FDI declined from 9 per cent to 4 per cent and that of manufacturing fell from 42 per cent to 29 per cent.

Offshoring and outsourcing of services abroad by firms in developed and developing countries have been contributing to this shift. The gradual liberalization of services industries, privatization, the dominance of M&As as the preferred source of financing and the increasing drive by firms to build on cost competitiveness have further strengthened the growth of FDI in services. As the transnationalization of the services sector in home and host countries lags behind that of manufacturing, there is scope for a further shift towards services.

There has been significant shift to FDI in the services sector

Outsourcing drives service sector FDI

Figure III.4.
Outward stock of global foreign direct investment, by sector, 1990 and 2002

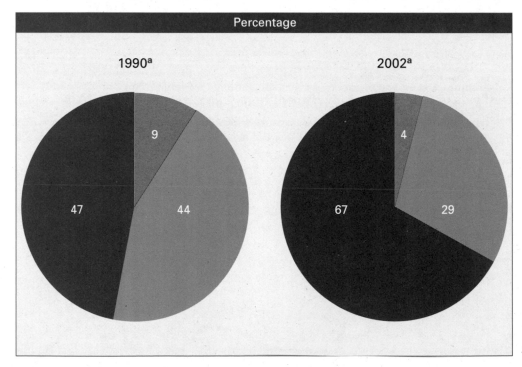

Manufacturing

Primary

Services

Source:
UNCTAD, *World Investment Report 2004: The Shift towards Services*, figure I.18.
Note:
In calculating the shares of the respective sectors, amounts recorded under "Private buying and selling of property" and "Unspecified" are excluded from the totals.

a   Or latest year available.

Outward FDI in services continues to be dominated by developed countries, but has become more evenly distributed among them (see table A.9). A few decades ago, most of the outward stock of FDI in services was held by firms from the United States. By 2002, Japan and the EU had emerged as significant sources of FDI in services. Outward FDI in services by developing countries began to grow visibly from the 1990s, with their share of the global stock of outward FDI in services climbing from 1 per cent in 1990 to 10 per cent in 2002, faster than in other sectors. Indian services firms lead in outward investment in business processing operations, call centres and information technology (IT) services. Firms in other developing economies are following suit in such areas as tourism, construction and telecommunications. Trade and trade-supporting services by manufacturing TNCs have expanded rapidly, while business services, hotels and restaurants, and financial services have also grown.

On the inward side, the distribution of the stock of FDI in services has been more balanced, although developed countries still account for the largest share—an estimated 72 per cent, compared to 25 per cent for developing economies—with Central and Eastern Europe accounting for the balance. In 2002, the United States was the largest host economy in terms of the size of its inward FDI stock in services. The fastest growth has taken place in Western Europe and the United States, reflecting the fact that most FDI in services is market-seeking. With a few exceptions (such as China), countries in which FDI in services has grown have also strengthened their positions as home and host countries for other forms of FDI. There is, however, considerable variation in the share of services in the FDI of individual countries.

The composition of FDI in services is also changing (see table A.10). In 1990, it was concentrated in trade and finance, which together accounted for 59 per cent of flows, but this share fell to 35 per cent in 2002. Such industries as electricity, water, telecommunications and business services (including IT-enabled corporate services) are becoming more prominent. Between 1990 and 2002, for example, the stock of FDI in electric power generation and distribution rose 14-fold; in telecommunications, storage and transport 16-fold; and in business services ninefold.

The composition of services FDI is changing

This shift in FDI partly reflects the increasing role of services in production: by 2001 services accounted, on average, for 72 per cent of GDP in developed countries, 52 per cent in developing countries and 57 per cent in Central and Eastern Europe countries. Moreover, most services are not tradable (they need to be produced when and where they are consumed) so the principal way for firms to bring services to foreign markets is through FDI. In addition, countries have liberalized their FDI regimes for services, making larger inflows possible, especially in industries previously closed to foreign entry. Of particular importance has been the privatization of State-owned utilities in Latin America and the Caribbean and in Central and Eastern Europe.

Services play an increasing role in production

Traditionally, FDI in such services as banking, insurance and transportation was motivated by the desire of firms in these sectors to provide their services to the overseas affiliates of the manufacturing clients that they served in their domestic markets. This continues, but the pattern has been changing: service providers increasingly invest abroad in search of new clients to exploit their ownership advantages and to respond to competitive pressures. For host countries, domestic economic growth remains the principal attraction for FDI in non-tradable services. In directly tradable services, the main attractions are access to good information and communication technologies (ICT), sound institutional infrastructure and the availability of productive and well-trained personnel at competitive costs.

The shift towards services is also discernible in cross-border M&As. The propensity of TNCs to enter new markets through M&As, rather than greenfield FDI, is much greater in such service industries as banking, telecommunications and water. In the late 1980s, services accounted for some 40 per cent of cross-border M&As, but this share rose to more than 60 per cent by the end of the 1990s. During the second half of the 1990s, most M&As took place in services and became a widely used mode of TNC entry. Privatization programmes open to FDI, which peaked in many countries during the 1990s, added to the number of M&As. Until the 1980s, cross-border M&As were almost exclusively the domain of United States TNCs, but TNCs from the EU have become the dominant actors, accounting for 61 per cent of all M&As in 2001-2003. Cross-border M&As have also played a prominent role in the overseas expansion of services TNCs based in developing countries.

There are signs that international production of services is evolving in a direction similar to that of international goods production. In the United States, for instance, the share of intra-firm imports in total imports of "other private services" rose from 30 per cent in 1986 to 47 per cent in 2002. To the extent that TNCs in the services sector are pursuing integrated strategies, however, they are "simple" rather than "complex" strategies, although some services TNCs have world product mandates for foreign affiliates (e.g., accounting services for a corporate system as a whole), as do simultaneous international production networks (such as when affiliates in various countries work on a common Research and development (R&D) project at the same time).

The growth of "outsourcing" and "offshoring" (see table III.6 for definitions) has also contributed to the shift of FDI towards services. These relatively new phenomena are small in value compared with FDI and involve firms from both developed and developing countries. Outsourcing and offshoring of services in such areas as business processing operations, shared services and call centres have been driven by the desire of firms to rationalize their activities and to reduce costs. The advances in ICT have also made these services tradable, that is to say, capable of being produced in one location and consumed elsewhere. The implication of this "tradability revolution" is that the production of entire service products (or parts thereof) can be distributed internationally—in countries other than a firm's home country—in line with the comparative advantages of individual loca-

Table III.6.

Some definitions of offshoring and outsourcing

Internalized or externalized production		
Location of production	Internalized	Externalized ("outsourcing")
Home country	Production kept in-house at home	Production outsourced to third party provider at home
Foreign country ("offshoring")	Production by foreign affiliate ("intra-firm (captive) offshoring")	Production outsourced to third party provider abroad: To local company To foreign affiliate of another TNC

tions and the competitive strategy of the firm. For these reasons, offshoring of services represents the cutting edge of the global shift in production activity, giving rise to a new international division of labour in the production of services, and is expected to grow rapidly.

International financial cooperation
Official flows

A year relatively free of financial crises was reflected in a significant fall in International Monetary Fund (IMF) lending in 2004. During the first nine months, the IMF was a net recipient of $8.7 billion from developing countries, as the volume of loan repayments exceeded IMF disbursements. The IMF was last in this position in 2000. The net flow of IMF resources in 2004 also reflected, to a certain extent, the level of commitments in 2003, and similarly, net flows in 2005 will reflect the fall in commitments in 2004. Total approved IMF commitments to the developing countries for the first nine months of the year slowed to a trickle at $1.1 billion, embodied in seven arrangements, compared to $17.6 billion in 18 arrangements for the entire 2003.

    Fund commitments to the economies in transition rose in 2004, albeit from only $0.2 billion in 2003 to $1.4 billion in the first nine months of 2004. Nevertheless, these countries have been transferring funds, on a net basis, to the IMF since 1999. With the European Bank for Reconstruction and Development (EBRD) assuming a larger role as provider of finance, IMF disbursements to these countries slowed in previous years and repayments have consistently exceeded new loans.

Official financial flows fell in 2004 in the absence of financial crises

Official development assistance

Data on total official development assistance (ODA) for 2004 are not yet available, but on the basis of total ODA of $69 billion recorded for 2003, the Development Assistance Committee (DAC) of the Organization for Economic Cooperation and Development (OECD) is projecting that the international donor community will provide some $77 billion in ODA in 2006, an increase of about one third, in real terms, over the total recorded in 2002. The rise in ODA is the result of the continued delivery on pledges to increase ODA made by donors at the International Conference on Financing for Development, held in Monterrey, Mexico, in March 2002. The EU and its member states will continue to be the major source of aid, generating well over half of all ODA. The United States is to raise ODA by $5 billion a year through 2006, which means a 50 per cent increase in core development assistance over that reached in 2002. The increased aid will be credited to a Millennium Challenge Account (MCA) to be disbursed through the newly created Millennium Challenge Corporation (MCC). The United States has released a list of 16 countries eligible to apply for assistance from the MCC in fiscal year 2005, and countries eligible to apply for Threshold Program Funding.[5]

    Notwithstanding the increase in official assistance since 2002, current ODA levels still fall far short of various estimates of the annual amount deemed necessary to achieve the Millennium Development Goals. Moreover, for the many poorer countries facing severe challenges, it is essential that most, if not all, assistance flows should be in the

Increases in ODA are expected to continue through 2006 ...

... but ODA will still fall short of ensuring success in meeting the Millennium Development Goals

form of grants. Grant finance, which declined in the 1990s, seems to be recovering. The negotiations for the replenishment of resources of the International Development Association (IDA), the World Bank's concessional lending window, for the lending period 1 July 2002-30 June 2005, or IDA-13, envisaged a larger share of assistance in the form of grants, and it is hoped that IDA-14 negotiations, which will cover the period 1 July 2005-30 June 2008, will reflect a continued increase in the provision of grants. A substantial and timely funding of IDA-14 will be a critical affirmation of the commitment of the international community to mobilizing the resources for its support of strong, results-oriented action by partners in the poorest countries.[6]

The composition of ODA is important in meeting the Millennium Development Goals

Furthermore, the ODA figures have to be interpreted with some caution. For example, when adjusted for depreciation of the US dollar and price inflation, the 18.4 per cent annual increase of ODA reported for 2003 relative to 2002 falls to around a quarter of that figure. In addition, it is normally expected that ODA should provide new cash resources that makes it possible for recipient countries to increase development spending. However an increasing portion of the recent increases in ODA has taken the form of expenditures on international security and emergency distress relief. Corrected for these items[7] reported by DAC for Afghanistan and Iraq, ODA in 2003 increased by a little over 1 per cent in real terms, suggesting that any increase in real resources to meet internationally agreed development objectives has been modest at best.

Official development cooperation

Efforts have been made to increase the quality of official development assistance ...

In addition to efforts to increase ODA levels to achieve the Millennium Development Goals and honour the Monterrey Consensus, efforts have been made to enhance aid effectiveness through better harmonization of aid procedures and improved coordination of donor policies and procedures. For instance, the Development Assistance Committee Working Party on Aid Effectiveness and Task Team on Harmonization and Alignment are acting to implement the commitments of the Rome high-level forum.[8] The Development Committee of the World Bank and the IMF, in its Communiqué of 2 October 2004, fully endorsed these agreements and called for the development of indicators and benchmarks to monitor the participation of all partners in this effort at the country level.[9]

... but much remains to be done

The Second International Roundtable on Managing for Development Results was held in Marrakech, Morocco, in February 2004 to help foster consensus on the priorities for the global partnership on managing for results. Sponsoring agencies have endorsed a joint memorandum, core principles and an action plan that can serve as a foundation to broaden this consensus and take further action in coming years. In addition, the staff of the World Bank and IMF prepared a report on aid effectiveness and financing modalities for the Development Committee meeting in October 2004 to address issues, including the role of aid, ongoing work on aid effectiveness, absorptive capacity and innovative financing mechanisms. Despite progress in increasing aid flows and improving aid harmonization and policy coordination among partners, the report concludes that much remains to be done. It notes the slow progress in improving overall aid practices, stating that a large gap exists between statements on the need to improve aid delivery, for instance, and the necessary actions by donors.[10]

Regional initiatives on aid effectiveness have been initiated

Aid effectiveness is also being addressed at the regional level. The European Commission, for instance, has put forward proposals aimed at expediting progress on the pledges made at the Barcelona Summit to achieve closer coordination of policies and harmonization of aid procedures of EU member States.[11] The Economic Commission for Africa (ECA) is engaged in a joint effort with DAC to create an institutional framework for mutual accountability between Africa and its partners. An important function of this alliance is to conduct joint Africa/DAC reviews of the impact of partner country policies on Africa's development cooperation programmes.

Concerns about the poor prospects of many sub-Saharan countries for attaining the Millennium Development Goals have also led the United Kingdom to launch a Commission for Africa with the objective of improving progress towards the internationally-agreed development goals in the region. In their consultations with the Commission, East African countries called for stronger support for such structures as the African Union and its development plan for Africa.[12] Calls for debt cancellation for African countries, the removal of trade-distorting subsidies, and the implementation of land redistribution programmes were also made.

New and innovative sources of development finance

Achieving the Millennium Development Goals by 2015 will require not only changes in policies and priorities but also a major effort by developing countries and the international community to mobilize additional financial resources. In its five-year review of the implementation of the outcome of the World Summit for Social Development, the General Assembly called for a rigorous analysis of the implications of proposals for developing new and innovative sources of development finance (resolution A/RES/S-24/2 of 1 July 2000). Paragraph 44 of the Monterrey Consensus also called on Member States and the United Nations Secretariat to pursue investigation of innovative sources of finance. In response, the Secretary-General commissioned the World Institute for Development Economics Research of the United Nations University (UNU-WIDER) to undertake a study of new and innovative sources of development finance. The purpose of the study was not to devise new financing mechanisms but to consider some of the better known existing proposals,[13] focusing on their design and policy implementations. The results of the study were published in 2004 and a summary was presented to the General Assembly.[14]

A number of other initiatives have responded to this call to seek ways to provide resources in addition to those generated by commitments of member States to achieve the Monterrey Consensus goal of 0.7 per cent of gross national income (GNI) in official development assistance. In November 2003, a group of independent experts was formed at the request of President Chirac of France to seek means by which the increased prosperity produced by globalization might be channelled into new financial contributions to create more and better funding for development purposes. The report of the group[15] surveyed a wide range of alternatives and provided a technical analysis of their feasibility without making specific recommendations.

In January 2004, the presidents of Brazil, Chile and France, together with the United Nations Secretary-General, launched an initiative, later endorsed by the President of the Government of Spain, to combat hunger and poverty that included the formation of a Technical Group to explore new and innovative sources of development finance. The work of the Technical Group was intended to contribute to multilateral efforts to mobilize additional resources for development.[16] The Meeting of World Leaders on Action against Hunger and Poverty at United Nations Headquarters in September 2004 resulted in a Declaration that stressed the need to raise

Studies of innovative sources of development finance have been undertaken by UNU-WIDER ...

... and France

A meeting of world leaders endorsed action on hunger and poverty and improve development assistance levels by giving further attention to innovative mechanisms of financing, both private and public, compulsory and voluntary, in order to raise funds for the attainment of the Millennium Development Goals and ensure the long-term stability of foreign aid.[17] As a result of subsequent deliberations in the General Assembly, it was agreed that discussions on the issue should continue in the appropriate fora.[18]

Innovative finance is
also on the agenda
of the Development
Committee

At its annual meeting in October 2004, the Joint Ministerial Committee of the Boards of Governors of the World Bank and the International Monetary Fund on the Transfer of Real Resources to Developing Countries also discussed the needs for additional stable and predictable financing to help developing countries meet the Millennium Development Goals. The Committee took note of the Meeting of World Leaders and requested the Bank and the Fund to continue work on these issues and to report at the next meeting on proposals on how the various options for additional financing might be implemented.[19]

A wide range of
innovative sources is
under investigation

Among the possible sources of development funding studied in the various reports were global environmental taxes; financial transactions taxes; taxes on arms sales; use of special drawing rights (SDRs) for development purposes; the International Finance Facility; private donations for international development; affinity credit cards; a global lottery; global premium bonds; combating tax evasion; and mobilizing emigrant remittances for development. Among the various proposals, the International Finance Facility is designed to provide increased funding quickly by employing financing arrangements that would allow future aid commitments to be used before they were disbursed, the objective being to achieve the Millennium Development Goals by 2015. If adopted, it would be desirable if this facility could be complemented by actions to ensure that there is no decline in aid flows after 2015. Among the other proposals, the technical reports conclude that only financial transactions taxes and environmental taxes might provide large amounts of additional resources in the longer term. However, realizing the potential of such taxes would require the full agreement of, and compliance by, all countries and this might be difficult to achieve. On the other hand, a proposal to make a new allocation of special drawing rights has already garnered support among members of the IMF; the use of existing allocations or a new allocation for development purposes could provide sizeable amounts of resources.

While concerns have been expressed that these initiatives might reduce existing commitments to official assistance, all of the reports and discussions of the issue stress that the various proposals should be seen as strictly additional to the ODA commitments target under the Monterrey Consensus.

Heavily Indebted Poor Country (HIPC) Initiative and other debt-relief measures

HIPC progress
remains slow

As at December 2004, 15 countries had reached their "completion point", qualifying them for debt relief under the Heavily Indebted Poor Countries (HIPC) Initiative.[20] Another 12 countries had reached their "decision points", making them eligible to receive interim debt relief. The implementation of the Initiative thus continues to progress slowly, owing mainly to the difficulty that eligible countries have in complying with the conditions required to receive debt relief. Maintaining macroeconomic stability remains a challenge for the countries that are in the interim phase of the programme.

Total debt relief accorded to the 27 countries that have reached either "decision point" or the "completion point", together with other debt relief measures, represents a two thirds reduction in these countries' overall debt stock. The ratio of debt service to exports for these countries has declined to an average of 10 per cent.

Notwithstanding the increased resources that debt relief makes available, HIPC countries continue to face difficulties in reconciling the objectives of achieving and maintaining debt sustainability, promoting long-term growth and reducing poverty. This is because priority in the implementation of poverty reduction strategy papers (PRSPs) has to be given to spending in social sectors, especially education and health.[21] Indeed, in some cases countries have had to borrow to meet deficits created by these new expenditure commitments. Sustained poverty reduction and debt sustainability also require increased domestic investment in infrastructure and in production capacity in order to raise economic growth and accelerate development.[22]

Debt sustainability is also affected by vulnerability to external shocks. For a number of heavily indebted poor countries, shocks from collapses in principal exports, droughts and other natural disasters, and civil strife have led to unsustainable debt levels. Moreover, eight of the 11 countries that have not yet reached the "decision points" are in conflict or post-conflict situations. They have also accumulated large protracted arrears with the international financial institutions.

Debt relief through the HIPC Initiative has been interpreted by many to have been intended to provide an addition to the total volume of ODA. Following the introduction of HIPC in 1995, however, total ODA transfers to the HIPC countries declined and have not yet recovered, despite a rise in bilateral ODA flows after 2001. Aid in grant form rose by 31 per cent between 2000 and 2002 (and has increasingly replaced bilateral loans to HIPC countries), but this increase was almost totally due to debt forgiveness (amounting to more than $2 billion), rather than being additional ODA flows.

Recent commitments by some non-HIPC developing countries, notably India and the Libyan Arab Jamahiriya, to provide debt relief to HIPC countries have provided a welcome increase in overall creditor participation, but most commercial creditors have not indicated a willingness to participate in the enhanced HIPC Initiative. Mobilizing the participation of these creditors remains a challenge to the international community.

The Paris Club group of creditor countries has continued to play an active role in the HIPC process. In October, Ethiopia's Paris Club creditors finalized the cancellation of $758 million in net present value terms of July 2003 representing the Paris Club's share of the effort in the framework of the Enhanced HIPC Initiative. Most creditors also committed on a bilateral basis to grant additional debt relief to Ethiopia so that the stock of the debt owed to Paris Club creditors will be reduced by a further $176 million in net present value terms of July 2003. In total, Ethiopia's debt to Paris Club creditors has been reduced from $1,087 million to $153 million in Net Present Value (NPV) terms of July 2003.

In November, Madagascar's Paris Club creditors agreed to recommend to their Governments a cancellation of $752 million in nominal terms ($292 million in NPV terms as of January 2000) which represents the Paris Club's corresponding share of the effort in the framework of the Enhanced HIPC Initiative. Most creditors also committed on a bilateral basis to grant substantial additional debt relief to Madagascar so that the stock of the debt owed to Paris Club creditors will be reduced by a further $699 million in nominal terms ($466 million in NPV). When finally approved, Madagascar's debt to Paris Club creditors will have been reduced from $1,572 million to $121 million as a result of this agreement and additional bilateral assistance.

The Paris Club has also been active in support of post-conflict countries. In November 2004, an agreement was reached on debt reduction of $38.9 billion out of its total foreign debt of $120 billion owed by Iraq to Paris Club creditors. The programme will initially provide cancellation of interest arrears equal to $11.6 billion in January

Debt sustainability is proving elusive in post-HIPC countries

External shocks and internal conflict hinder access for many countries

HIPC has not produced the expected additionality to ODA

Developing countries also participate in HIPC as donors

The Paris Club support of HIPC remains crucial

Paris Club has also provided support for post-conflict countries ...

2005. The remaining reduction will be deferred until approval of an IMF standard adjustment programme when a further reduction of $11.6 billion will be made. An additional debt reduction of $7.8 billion of the initial debt stock will be granted when the last review of the three-year implementation of the IMF adjustment programme is completed. The total debt reduction agreed will reduce Iraq's outstanding debt stock to Paris Club creditors to $7.8 billion. The remainder of the debt will be rescheduled over 23 years with a grace period of 6 years. The agreement is expected to serve as a benchmark for other creditors, including Saudi Arabia and Kuwait, which hold the bulk of the debt, and some Eastern European countries.

In December, Paris Club creditors agreed with the Government of the Republic of the Congo to a restructuring of its public external debt, following the approval of an arrangement under the Poverty Reduction and Growth Facility by the IMF in December 2004. This agreement treats a total amount of $3,020 million of debt, cancelling $1,680 million and rescheduling $1,340 million. This amount consists of arrears (including late interest) as of 30 September 2004 and of maturities falling due from 1 October 2004 up to 30 September 2007. The agreement is concluded under Naples terms.

... and is considering relief for Asian debtors hit by the tsunami

In early January 2005, Paris Club creditors agreed that, consistent with the national laws of the creditor countries, requests for relief from debt payments by countries affected by the tsunami of 26 December 2004 would be granted until the World Bank and the IMF had made a full assessment of these countries' reconstruction and financing needs. In the light of that assessment, which is expected to take two to three months, creditors will consider what further steps are necessary, with the response being determined by the situation of each country.

Multilateral surveillance

Efforts are under way to strengthen IMF surveillance activities

Effective and even-handed surveillance by the Fund of all its members remains the major tool for crisis prevention and the promotion of orderly international financial relations. In July 2004, the IMF Executive Board concluded its latest biennial review of surveillance activities and identified several measures to further strengthen surveillance.[23] It has been agreed that surveillance should be focused on exchange-rate policies, financial sector stability, external and fiscal sustainability, the global repercussions of the national policies of the major developed countries and the closer integration of multilateral, regional and bilateral surveillance. It has also been recognized that the surveillance process should promote a frank and continuous dialogue between the Fund and its members, build trust with the national authorities and strengthen communication of the Fund's policy messages.

Identifying reasons for non-compliance is as important as the surveillance

According to some observers, a shortcoming of the biennial review was that it focused mainly on the process of surveillance rather than on an assessment of the Fund's effectiveness in assisting countries to implement appropriate policies. Fund surveillance can be effective only if members are ready to listen and policy recommendations therefore prompt timely action. In determining the future direction of surveillance, it is therefore deemed more important to pay attention to identifying why a country is not following Fund recommendations than to evaluating the relevance and appropriateness of past advice.

The timing and intensity of surveillance are important

To raise the effectiveness of surveillance, greater selectivity and increased focus on country-specific areas of vulnerability are also considered necessary. Consequently, more attention should be paid to identifying not only the specific objectives of surveillance in the light of the circumstances facing the country concerned, but also the appropriate timing and intensity of surveillance. This requires surveillance that is tailor-made to addressing mainly those macroeconomic issues that are relevant in each member country. Better alignment of surveillance with country circumstances, including the stage of economic and financial market development, requires national authorities to be more active in determining the main thrust of Fund surveillance in their countries. This includes providing guidance to the Fund on areas where its activities would be most beneficial.

Policy discussions should also adequately capture the country's own development priorities, institutional setting, and political economy and should strive to examine alternative options for attaining a specified objective. To ensure that reforms are growth-oriented, more emphasis should be given to the "qualitative" adjustment achieved through the pursuit of "quantitative" objectives.

It has been argued that the restrictions on overall levels of government expenditures in the pursuit of sound economic fundamentals have been one of the reasons for the lack of infrastructure investment in developing countries. It is thus imperative to formulate policies that produce sound macroeconomic fundamentals compatible with substantial increases in investment in human capital and social and economic overhead capital.

Sound macroeconomic fundamentals should not be such as to deter infrastructure investment

In this regard, the design of appropriate fiscal rules has received a great deal of attention in recent years. For instance, work is under way in the Fund on the treatment of public investment and, more generally, the design of fiscal policy in surveillance and Fund programmes. The IMF is conducting a number of pilot studies in Latin America and other parts of the world to evaluate more flexible approaches to public investment in infrastructure. The results of these studies are expected to provide the basis for recommendations on when and how to relax constraints on borrowing to finance public investment without jeopardizing macroeconomic stability and debt sustainability.[24]

Another dimension of surveillance effectiveness is the extent of institutional capacities in countries. Consequently, the provision of technical assistance for capacity-building should be an integral part of the effort to reduce vulnerabilities and support the implementation of reforms. It may be necessary to devote more resources to this kind of assistance, demand for which continues to grow.

There have been proposals to introduce a Policy Monitoring Arrangement (PMA) in the Fund for countries that do not need a borrowing arrangement but want to strengthen their surveillance relationship or obtain, for the benefit of markets and donors, the IMF's assessment of the strength of their policies.[25] Such an instrument is seen by its proponents as necessary to fill the gap between surveillance and financial programmes. However, critics of the new arrangements question the benefits of creating for signalling purposes an instrument such as the proposed PMA, which includes upper credit tranche conditionality without Fund financing. Extending the principles of programme reviews and monitoring to policy assessments and reviews in non-programme countries for signaling purposes is seen by critics as counterproductive. It is argued that such an instrument would be less effective than existing precautionary arrangements that allow countries to borrow in case of need. Also, there are concerns that the proposed PMA may not only become a requirement for lending, grants and debt relief, but may also substitute for existing facilities by minimizing lending to low-income countries.[26]

A proposed Policy Monitoring Arrangement raises questions

It has thus been suggested that, instead of creating a new instrument, it would be more productive to concentrate on more efficient and flexible use of the untapped potential of the existing mechanisms, particularly Article IV Consultations. Before further discussions on the PMA, it would be useful to determine the extent of the demand for such a mechanism among members, and whether markets or donors need the proposed IMF signalling.

Precautionary financial arrangements

The need for new
instruments to fight
financial crisis is
under discussion

Effective surveillance, strong regulation and supervision, and sound economic policies do not eliminate the risk of a capital-account crisis. Consequently, there is a need for insurance in the form of foreign exchange liquidity for countries with sound policies to cope with potential capital-account crises stemming from sudden changes in capital flows. The Contingent Credit Line (CCL) was intended to provide such insurance, but was never used and expired in November 2003. Since then, the IMF has been exploring other ways to achieve this objective. In particular, there have been discussions on the possibility of adapting an existing instrument—namely, the stand-by precautionary arrangements[27] that are typically used when balance-of-payments pressures are likely to arise in the current account—to the needs of countries facing a potential capital-account shock.[28]

Are existing provisions
sufficient ...

There is a consensus that precautionary arrangements within normal access limits have been reasonably successful in providing support for members' strong policies. However, views differ on whether the structure of the precautionary arrangements should be modified to allow the use of exceptional access under such arrangements.[29] The opponents of such a modification note that the promotion of sound policies is the best form of crisis prevention, and the precautionary arrangements with normal access limits have been successful because the focus of the programme has been on the implementation of the necessary policy adjustments to reduce vulnerabilities. Accordingly, the extension of the policy to cover precautionary arrangements with exceptional access may change the emphasis from promoting policy adjustments to financing capital-account crises, thus exacerbating moral hazard issues. It has also been argued that the precautionary commitment of significant resources may constrain the ability of the Fund to respond to an actual crisis.

... or are new
mechanisms necessary
to prevent capital
account crises?

The alternative view is that the absence of effective insurance against capital-account crises is an important gap in the tools available for crisis prevention. According to this view, precautionary exceptional access could significantly strengthen the Fund's role in crisis prevention. A new policy would provide greater assurances to the member and to financial markets of the availability of Fund support and should reduce the probability of crisis by boosting market confidence. Moral hazard issues associated with such a facility are considered to be exaggerated as empirical support is not sufficient or lacking.

In addition, by bringing access more in line with the potential need, a modified facility is expected to encourage more countries to adopt strong policies. It is also argued that the inadequacy of the "collective" insurance provided by the existing Fund facilities has forced developing countries to build up their own "self insurance" either in the form of excessive reserve accumulation or by devising alternative regional funding mechanisms to insulate themselves from external shocks. However, such "self-insurance" is not cost efficient when sub-optimal provision of emergency liquidity financing leads to contractionary economic policies to support excessive reserve accumulation and generates a contractionary bias for the world economy.

These different points of view, related in many cases to fundamental issues pertaining to the role of the Fund, are unlikely to be bridged soon. Nevertheless, there remains a need for the further exploration of financing mechanisms to help prevent capital-account crises. Efforts should continue to reach agreement on the general direction of such exploration.

Crisis resolution

There has been some progress towards establishing voluntary mechanisms for the orderly and cost-efficient resolution of financial crises. The inclusion of Collective Action Clauses (CACs) in sovereign bond issues has gained greater acceptance and, contrary to earlier expectations in some quarters, has not had an adverse impact on the cost of issuance. As of the end of September 2004, more than 40 per cent of the value of the outstanding stock of international sovereign bonds issued by emerging market countries included CACs.[30] However, it will be possible to assess the relevance of CACs for an orderly debt restructuring process only when they have to be applied in practice.

Some sovereign debtors and private creditors have been attempting to develop voluntary "Principles of Stable Capital Flows and Fair Debt Restructuring in Emerging Markets", but progress has been slow. At its November 2004 meeting, the Group of Twenty welcomed the work on such principles and stressed their importance for strengthening crisis prevention and enhancing predictability of crisis management.[31] Defining a framework that is sufficiently binding to be of practical use in a debt restructuring process, but remains voluntary, has proven difficult. It remains to be seen whether voluntary efforts, such as these principles, can provide a sufficiently strong basis for an effective crisis resolution mechanism.

Amid the limited progress on a framework for crisis resolution, policies on the provision of IMF resources in capital-account crises have come under scrutiny. The emergence of capital-account crises has sharply increased the need for the Fund resources and the burden of financing has increasingly been put on the IMF, while the decision-making process has tilted from rules to discretion. Setting strict limits to Fund financing may not be appropriate, as it may unnecessarily restrict the Fund's room for manoeuvre. On the other hand, the IMF should not be put in a position where it always has to fully offset private capital flows.

In 2002, to improve clarity and predictability of official responses to capital-account crises, IMF introduced a framework for exceptional access to its resources. In decisions on such access, the most important aspect is whether lending is justified at all, rather than the absolute amount of lending. According to the framework, the Fund may grant exceptional access to a country if three basic conditions are fulfilled: high probability that the debt will remain sustainable; good prospects of regaining access to private capital markets; and reasonable chances of success with the country's policy programme.

It has proven easier to define this framework than to implement it. Thus far, the new procedure has not reduced debtor countries' and market participants' heavy reliance on official financial support, while in many cases programmes have not been considered strong enough. In the assessment of the three required conditions, it is difficult to avoid a strong element of judgement, and hence political involvement. In addition, it is difficult to eliminate a bias towards excessive Fund financing because the alternative is often the prospect of a large-scale systemic crisis. According to many observers, recent cases of large and prolonged Fund lending have weakened the reputation of the Fund and put into question the effectiveness of its programmes in catalyzing private capital flows. It has also been argued that the current policies on crisis resolution remain tilted towards bailing out the private sector.

There have consequently been strong calls for the creation of clearer limits and criteria for exceptional access and for rigorous adherence to them. Strict adherence to the rules governing exceptional access is deemed necessary to secure predictable financial crisis

Some voluntary mechanisms have been implemented ...

... and discussions on a set of voluntary principles continue

The extent of IMF support remains under discussion

More clarity on exceptional access to IMF support ....

... has not made implementation easier ...

... and has led to further discussion of access criteria

management, ensure equal treatment of member states, encourage involvement of the private sector in the resolution of crises, reduce creditor and debtor moral hazard, and safeguard the resources of the Fund and the credibility of its policies. It has also been stressed that, in exceptional access cases, financial assistance from the Fund should only support sound policies, even when that requires a significant policy shift. It seems, however, that a stronger framework for exceptional access will not be enough to involve the private sector, and the development of other tools may be necessary. Progress in this respect has been disappointingly slow.

In this regard, the existing instrument, the Fund's policy for lending into arrears, could be used more effectively to involve the private sector more consistently in the resolution of crises and thereby in burden-sharing. According to this policy, the Fund may lend into arrears if a country makes a significant policy adjustment in an effort to resolve arrears and if it engages in negotiations with its private creditors in good faith to restore debt sustainability. The policy could be improved by clearer and more operational criteria for judging "good faith", including specification of the key elements of a constructive dialogue.

Financial regulation and supervision

The reform of Basel capital adequacy regulations is nearing completion

After nearly six years of work, the text of a new capital framework for banking organizations (Basel II) was published in June 2004. The proposal is currently being evaluated by national bank supervisory authorities. In some countries, this includes additional field tests to provide a better understanding of how the implementation of a more risk-sensitive approach for regulatory capital standards might affect minimum required capital at the industry, institution and portfolio level. Also, for an extended period of time, banks in all G10 countries will calculate their capital requirements under both the old 1988 Accord and the new Basel II framework. These additional field tests and parallel calculations are aimed to serve as the final checks of Basel II prior to its implementation. Because of the need for additional assessments of the impact of the new framework, the end of the transition period for implementation of the more advanced proposed approaches for G10 countries has been moved from the end of 2006 to the end of 2008. More time is also considered necessary to clarify and provide supplementary guidance for some of the rules, and additional work is needed to foster greater consistency in the implementation and application of the new framework across countries.

Developing countries are exempt from the implementation schedule

There is no implementation timetable for non-G10 countries. It has been recognized that, because of its complexity, Basel II will probably not be adopted as widely and quickly as the 1988 Accord[32] and that, given the national resource and other constraints facing many developing countries, there may be more immediate regulatory concerns that need to be tackled before Basel II implementation.[33] The new system will have substantial implementation costs, which many developing countries would have to divert from other uses. In particular, some issues of concern to developing countries—such as the procyclicality of regulatory arrangements and international portfolio diversification—were not adequately dealt with in Basel II, and developing countries may wish to give higher priority to building stronger and deeper domestic financial systems. Nevertheless, many developing and emerging market countries have already begun to deal with implementation issues and it is expected that, by 2010, over 90 per cent of banking assets in the developing world will be covered by Basel II arrangements.[34]

International standards and codes

The major focus regarding standards and codes has been on improving implementation, since a great deal of practical experience has now been accumulated. Over two thirds of IMF member countries had completed or committed to undertake at least one module of a Report on the Observance of Standards and Codes (ROSC) as of end June 2004[35] and over 80 country Financial Sector Assessment Programme (FSAP) reviews had been completed or were under way as of September 2004.[36] Previous reviews recommended reducing the number of FSAPs and putting greater focus on follow-up and adjustment to country circumstances.

At its twelfth meeting in September 2004, the Financial Stability Forum (FSF) discussed a paper prepared by the IMF that described gaps in the implementation of standards and raised a number of issues relating to the standards themselves, [37] in particular the shortage of internationally-agreed capital and risk management standards in the insurance sector.

The FSF considered ways to improve the implementation of regulatory standards in the banking, securities and insurance sectors, based on the experience of the FASP. It discussed the treatment of preconditions for the effective implementation of standards, the consistency of the implementation methodology, cross-sector and cross-border regulation, regulatory and corporate governance, especially for State-owned enterprises (SOEs), and public disclosure. The FSF concluded by encouraging international standard-setting bodies to consider cross-sector issues with a view to addressing inconsistencies and incompatibilities among the standards in different financial sectors.[38]

Meanwhile, collaborative efforts of the World Bank and the United Nations Commission on International Trade Law (UNCITRAL) are under way to develop a unified international standard for insolvency and creditor rights that takes into account different legal traditions. At its November 2004 meeting, the G-20 stressed the importance of this work.[39]

In the area of corporate governance, the OECD Steering Group on Corporate Governance is developing an assessment methodology for the OECD's revised Corporate Governance Principles that were approved in May 2004. The OECD is also working on governance guidelines for SOEs in consultation with non-OECD countries.

The international coherence of work to strengthen financial reporting and governance remains a pressing issue. At its September 2004 meeting, the FSF discussed developments regarding International Financial Reporting Standards (IFRS) and the progress towards convergence between the International Accounting Standards Board (IASB) and the United States Financial Accounting Standards Board (FASB). The Forum noted that attention needed to shift to effective implementation of IFRS standards. The Forum also noted that the standards regarding audit quality and auditor oversight are used by many countries and more would adopt them in 2005 alongside the move to IFRS. For instance, all listed EU companies will have to use these IFRS from 2005.

In September 2004, the Board of the International Federation of Accountants (IFAC) published a study in which it recommended further actions to achieve convergence to international standards. An important element of the IFAC study was the identification of challenges faced by small and medium-sized entities and accounting firms, including those working in developing countries, in implementing the standards.[40] In July 2004, the IFAC Board established a working group to organize an international summit on small and medium practice (SMP) issues in early 2005.

The implementation of standards and codes is well advanced

Discussions are under way to improve financial sector standards

Proposals for improving corporate governance are being developed

International accounting standards also under discussion

IFAC also formed a partnership with UNCTAD to identify the needs of developing and transition economies in their efforts to meet the International Education Standards addressing accounting education and professional qualifications, as well as to assist them in the implementation of best practices of corporate governance. The IFAC Developing Nations Permanent Task Force provides support to the development of the accountancy profession in these countries. The Task Force is to work with the IFAC Compliance Program to respond to the needs of developing countries, including accessing resources within the IFAC membership and donors.

The Public Sector Committee (PSC) of the IFAC reported in July 2004 that its survey of the views of stakeholders confirmed the overwhelming support for an independent standard setter for international public sector financial reporting standards. It was recommended that the PSC be renamed the "International Public Sector Accounting Standards Board".[41]

In March 2004, the IMF and World Bank endorsed the revision of the Financial Action Task Force's FATF 40+8 Recommendations as the revised standard for Anti-Money Laundering/Combating the Financing of Terrorism (AML/CFT) assessments, under which 30 to 40 assessments are expected to be conducted annually. At its November 2004 meeting, the G-20 reiterated its commitment to implement the revised FATF Forty Recommendations and the FATF Special Recommendations and welcomed the decision by the IMF and the World Bank to make comprehensive assessments on money laundering and terrorist financing a regular part of their work.

Voice and participation of developing countries in the Bretton Woods Institutions

Progress in improving voice and participation has slowed

Voice and effective participation are issues that go to the centre of the international financial institutions' legitimacy, relevance and effectiveness. The Monterrey Consensus stressed "...the need to broaden and strengthen the participation of developing countries and economies in transition in international economic decision-making and norm setting".[42] Since then, a number of proposals have been put forward, but there has been no progress in deciding how to change the quotas, capital shares and voting rights of member countries to reflect the evolution of different economies and to correct the underrepresentation of the developing countries in the decision-making processes of the IMF and the World Bank. However, exercises based on adjustment to existing formulae for representation have been shown to produce only marginal changes in representation, and not all of them provide for improvement in representation of developing countries.

Discussion continues at the IMF and World Bank

At their meetings in October 2004, the International Monetary and Financial Committee and the Development Committee took note of a status report[43] regarding work on voice and participation, and asked the Boards of the IMF and World Bank to consider these issues further. While the Executive Board discussions can be useful in elaborating the details of various proposals for change within existing parameters, real changes in representation can only be achieved through fundamental reform that has to come from political leaders.

Notes

1   The net financial transfer statistic adds together receipts of foreign investment income and financial inflows from abroad minus payments of foreign investment income and financial outflows, including increases in foreign reserve holdings. The net financial transfer of a country is thus the financial counterpart to the balance of trade in goods and services. A trade surplus is generated when the total value of domestic production exceeds domestic consumption and investment, with the excess invested abroad, and vice versa for a trade deficit.

2   Eight countries acceded to the European Union in 2004. They are the Czech Republic, Estonia, Hungary, Latvia, Lithuania, Poland, Slovakia and Slovenia.

3   A single transaction of nearly $20 billion involving an intra-company loan by a telecommunications company accounted for almost half the total recorded outflow of foreign capital of $42.7 billion from Germany in the first half of 2004.

4   For a further analysis of this issue, see UNCTAD *World Investment Report 2004: The Shift Towards Services.*

5   The 16 countries are Armenia, Benin, Bolivia, Georgia, Ghana, Honduras, Lesotho, Madagascar, Mali, Mongolia, Morocco, Mozambique, Nicaragua, Senegal, Sri Lanka and Vanuatu. Morocco is eligible for the first time, while the other countries were also selected in fiscal year 2004. Cape Verde is no longer on the list. The countries that are eligible for the first time in the fiscal year 2005 Threshold Program are Burkina Faso, Guyana, Malawi, Paraguay, the Philippines and Zambia. Threshold countries are those that do not qualify for MCA assistance but have demonstrated a commitment to meeting the eligibility requirements for MCA assistance in the future.

6   In IDA-13, it was agreed that assistance in the form of grants would range from 18-21 per cent of total aid resources. In IDA-14, representatives have met four times in 2004. Civil society also participated in the discussions. The main issues discussed were debt sustainability to low income borrowers, the measurement of progress in IDA-financed projects and the volume of resources needed by IDA-eligible countries.

7   ODA at 2002 prices less assistance reported for Afghanistan and Iraq for 2002 ($968,394,000) and 2003 ($3,069,071,000) under headings 15061 Post-Conflict Peace Building, 16340 Reconstruction Relief, 71010 Emergency Food Aid, 72010 Emergency-Distress Relief and 72030 Aid to Refugees in Recipient Countries in the OECD/DAC Creditor Reporting System-1-CRS/Aid Activities—Commitments—All details : 1973-2003. Total ODA at 2002 prices reported for the two countries was $1,515,061,000 in 2002 and $7,395,247,000 in 2003

8   The High level Forum on Harmonization convened in Rome in February 2003 and resulted in the Rome Declaration. In the Declaration, participating countries pledged to, inter alia, better harmonize ODA procedures and to reduce "red tape", building on the commitments of the Monterrey Consensus. It led to the creation of the DAC Team on Harmonization and Alignment. Based on the indicators framework developed by the DAC Team, an OECD-DAC Survey on Progress in Harmonization and Alignment has been carried out in 14 countries (Bangladesh, Bolivia, Cambodia, Ethiopia, Fiji, Kyrgyzstan, Morocco, Mozambique, Nicaragua, Niger, Senegal, the United Republic of Tanzania, Viet Nam and Zambia) and the draft overview of the results of the survey has been released. The findings of the survey will be used to report progress to the Second High-Level Forum on Harmonization and Alignment of Aid Effectiveness in early 2005. See "Aid Effectiveness and Donor Practices: Results of the OECD-DAC Survey on Harmonization and Alignment (first draft)", 12 November 2004 (available from www.oecd.org/dac).

9   See International Monetary Fund and the World Bank, Development Committee, Communiqué, para.6, 2 October 2004 (available from http://siteresources.worldbank.org/DEVCOMMINT/NewsAndEvents/20264401/Sept_2004_DC_Communique_E.pdf).

10   See Development Committee, "Aid effectiveness and financing modalities", prepared by the staff of the World Bank and the International Monetary Fund, 28 September 2004 (available from http://siteresources.worldbank.org/DEVCOMMINT/Documentation/20264307/DC2004-0012(E)%20Aid%20Eff%20Add1.pdf).

11   See Commission of the European Communities, "Communication from the Commission to the Council…", p. 2.

12   See Voice of America News, "Commission for Africa wraps up consultations", Nairobi, 8 December 2004 (available from http://www.voanews.com).

13 See A.B. Atkinson (ed.), New Sources of Development Finance (Oxford, Oxford University Press, 2004).

14 See "Innovative sources of financing for development", note by the Secretary-General of the United Nations, 17 August 2004 (A/59/272).

15 *Les nouvelles contributions financières internationales,* Rapport au Président de la République du Groupe de travail présidé par Jean-Pierre Landau, Paris, La documentation Française, Septembre 2004.

16 See "Action against hunger and poverty: Report of the technical group on innovative financing mechanisms", September 2004.

17 See "Action against Hunger and Poverty, The New York Declaration on the Action against Hunger and Poverty", 20 September 2004, New York (available from http://www.mre.gov.br).

18 See General Assembly resolution A/RES/59/225.

19 See International Monetary Fund and the World Bank, Development Committee, Communiqué, para.9, 2 October 2004.

20 The countries are: Benin, Bolivia, Burkina Faso, Ethiopia, Ghana, Guyana, Madagascar, Mali, Mauritania, Mozambique, Nicaragua, Niger, Senegal, the Republic of Tanzania and Uganda.

21 It is estimated that, on average, 65 per cent of all resources released by HIPC debt relief until early 2003 has been devoted to the social sectors, compared to 7 per cent for infrastructure. See World Bank, Operations Evaluations Department, *Debt Relief for the Poorest: An OED Review of the HIC Initiative,* Washington D.C., 2003, p.34. Debt relief under the HIPC Initiative has helped countries to increase poverty-reducing expenditures from an average of 6.3 per cent of GDP in 1999 to 7.9 per cent of GDP in 2003. See International Monetary Fund and International Development Association, Heavily Indebted Poor Countries (HIPC) Initiative: Status of Implementation, prepared by the staff of the IMF and World Bank, 20 August 2004.

22 United Nations Conference on Trade and Development, *Trade and Development Report, 1997* (United Nations publication, Sales No. E.97.II.D.8), part two, chap.V.

23 "IMF Executive Board Reviews the Fund's Surveillance", Public Information Notice (PIN) No. 04/95, 24 August 2004 (available from http://www.imf.org).

24 For a discussion of possible new approaches to investment in infrastructure and other public projects, see, for instance, Richard Hemming and Teresa Ter-Minassian, "Possible new approaches to fiscal accounting", Finance & Development, December 2004, pp. 30-33.

25 Policy Development and Review Department, "Policy Monitoring Arrangement", IMF, 8 September 2004 (available from http://www.imf.org); "IMF Executive Board Discusses Policy Signaling Instrument", Public Information Notice (PIN) No. 04/114, 1 October 2004 (available from http://www.imf.org).

26 International Group of Twenty-Four on International Monetary Affairs and Development, Communiqué, 1 October 2004, p. 2 (available from http://www.g24.org).

27 Under these arrangements, the country does not draw upon the agreed amount of the Fund's resources unless economic circumstances deteriorate.

28 See, for instance, "IMF Discusses Status Report on Crisis Prevention and Precautionary Arrangements", Public Information Notice (PIN) No. 04/117, 6 October 2004 (available from http://www.imf.org).

29 Under current policies, exceptional access can be allowed only to support an *actual* balance of payments need stemming from pressures on the capital account.

30 "Progress Report to the International Monetary and Financial Committee on Crisis Resolution", IMF, 28 September 2004, p. 2 (available from http://www.imf.org).

31 See <http://www.g20.org>.

32 Jaime Caruana, "Basel II—emerging market perspectives", remarks for a panel discussion on "Basel II—emerging market perspectives", Bankers' Conference 2004, New Delhi, 11 November 2004 (available from http://www.bis.org).

33 The IMF and the World Bank will not base their FSAP assessments on Basel II if a country has elected not to implement it.

34 Malcolm Knight, "The vulnerability of emerging markets to shocks: what has changed since the mid-1990s?", speech at the Toronto Center Executive Forum, 9 November 2004 (available from http://www.bis.org).

35 Report of the Managing Director of the IMF to the International Monetary and Financial Committee, September 30, 2004.

36   Evaluation of the Financial Sector Assessment Program (FSAP), Issues Paper, 20 October 2004.

37   "Financial Sector Regulation: Issues and Gaps—An Update", IMF, 25 October 2004 (available from http://www.imf.org).

38   "Twelfth Meeting of the FSF (Washington, 8-9 September 2004), FSF Press Release (available from http://www.fsforum.org).

39   G-20 Communiqué, "Meeting of Finance Ministers and Central Bank Governors, Berlin, 20-21 November 2004" (available from http://www.g20.org).

40   "International Study Recommends Actions to Achieve Convergence to International Standards", IFAC news release, 3 November 2004 (available from http://www.ifac.org).

41   Helene Kennedy, "IFAC Board Focuses on Public Interest Issues and Needs of SMEs, Developing Nations", 14 July 2004 (available from http://www.ifac.org).

42   "Monterrey Consensus", Final Outcome of the International Conference on Financing for Development, adopted on 22 March 2002, para. 62.

43   "Voice and Participation of Developing and Transition Countries" (available from http://siteresources.worldbank.org/DEVCOMMINT/Documentation/20263399/DC2004-00014(E)-Voice.pdf).

Chapter IV
Regional developments and outlook

Developed market economies

North America: growing constraints for the United States

Growth in Canada and the United States averaged more than 4 per cent in 2004, but their combined increase in gross domestic product (GDP) is expected to fall to 3 per cent in 2005 (see table I.1) as performance is constrained by the unwinding of previous policy stimuli, higher oil prices, weak employment growth, mounting debt in the household sector and the United States twin deficits. While some resilience and flexibility remain, the United States economy, particularly the seemingly unflinching propensity of consumers to spend, may have become overstretched.

Much of the United States strong performance in 2004 was due to vigorous growth in the first quarter, but the expansion then slowed, particularly in the second quarter as consumer spending stalled and export growth decelerated (see figure IV.1). Although other weaknesses were also involved, the surge in oil prices was a major factor behind the modera-

Growth decelerates during the year as oil prices surge

Figure IV.1.
Growth of GDP in the EU-12, Japan and the United States, quarterly, 2002-2004

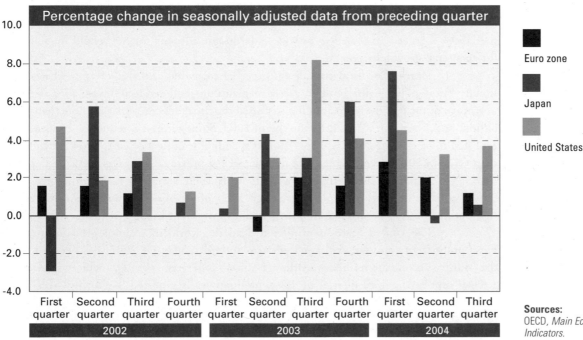

Euro zone

Japan

United States

Sources:
OECD, *Main Economic Indicators.*

tion. The rise in crude oil prices has not been fully passed through to the prices of gasoline and heating oil, and even less to the prices of other goods and services. As oil prices are expected to remain at their increased levels in 2005 (see chapter II), the adverse effects will likely accumulate: real disposable income and household spending will be further constrained and business profits will be squeezed. Growth is expected to decline to 3 per cent.

Consumption spending remains the economic driver as household savings hit record lows

Consumption spending has been the mainstay of the recovery in the United States, but at the cost of the household savings rate dropping to a record low of less than 1 per cent during 2004. This was partly due to higher oil prices as consumers maintained their real consumption by reducing savings. However, the decline in the saving rates over the past few years, and the associated consumer spending spree, was driven primarily by the appreciation of housing prices, low interest rates and the use of mortgage refinancing to finance consumption. As a result, household debt has reached a record high. The forecast projects housing prices to peak, if not decline, while interest rates, although remaining low, will continue to move upward in gradual steps. These two key sources of support for consumer spending are therefore expected to wane. Moreover, if interest rates were to rise more rapidly than anticipated, due either to an escalation of inflation driven by increased oil prices or to a sell-off of dollar-denominated assets by foreign investors, housing prices could fall more rapidly and the debt burden would squeeze consumer spending more severely.

Employment has yet to register a convincing upturn

The strength in the household sector will also depend on the recovery in employment. Employment growth had been exceptionally slow, but showed some strengthening in the fourth quarter of 2004. Nevertheless, the growth in payroll employment is averaging less than 200,000 per month, sufficient only to maintain a stable unemployment rate. In addition, there are some structural weaknesses underlying the aggregate number: government hiring has increased, but private sector job growth is below its historical average and manufacturing jobs continue to decline. Despite these constraints, further improvement in employment is expected in 2005 as a result of diminishing growth of productivity and increased business capital spending (see table A.1). However, with the current unemployment rate of 5.5 per cent, compared to the low of around 4 per cent reached in 2000, and taking into account the deterioration in the labour force participation rate, the labour market is expected to provide only meagre support for household income and for economic growth in general.

The stimulus from fiscal policy will be withdrawn

Meanwhile, fiscal stimuli are expected to dwindle, if not reverse. The expansionary fiscal policy, with both increased expenditure and reduced taxes, alleviated the downturn of the past few years, but it also caused the fiscal deficit to soar to more than $400 billion, or 3.5 per cent of GDP, by the end of 2004. Some of the tax reduction measures are expected to be extended, but real government spending is not expected to grow much faster than GDP in 2005, decelerating from the pace of the previous two years.

While the fiscal stimulus will diminish, there are a few favourable forces that should provide a boost: high productivity growth, robust business investment, low inflation and, possibly, a stronger-than-anticipated improvement in employment.

Productivity growth decelerates but remains strong

The United States continues to lead the world in technological innovation. High productivity growth, about 4.5 per cent in both 2002 and 2003, has been a key to the country's economic resilience. Although it has moderated recently, including a drop to 1.9 per cent in the third quarter of 2004, productivity is expected to grow by over 2 per cent for the next few years, implying a potential growth rate for the economy of about 3 to 3.5 per cent.

Business investment remains strong, boosted by improving corporate profits, low interest rates and a recovery in equity prices. The scheduled expiration at the end of 2004 of the tax provision to encourage capital depreciation contributed to the acceleration in business investment in 2004, but is expected to slow investment spending in early 2005. Renewed growth of business investment is expected thereafter.

Despite the increase in oil prices, the rate of inflation, as measured by the consumer price index (CPI), rose only to 2.6 per cent in 2004, from 2.3 per cent in 2003. Meanwhile, inflationary expectations, as measured by the difference in yields on inflation-indexed government bonds and conventional government bonds, have also edged up only slightly. This benign inflation outlook enabled the Federal Reserve (Fed) to adopt a gradual tightening of monetary policy, with five quarter-point increases in interest rates to 2¼ per cent by the end of 2004. In the forecast, it is assumed that the Fed will continue to raise policy interest rates further, to 3.5 per cent by the end of 2005. Even at that level, real interest rates will remain below their historical average (see figure IV.2).

Economic growth in Canada has accelerated since the second quarter of 2004, driven by both strong external demand and an improvement in the terms of trade. However, there are also some countervailing forces, such as the appreciated currency, rising interest rates, and the high dependency on demand from the United States and other countries. GDP is projected to grow by 2¾ per cent in 2005, the same pace as in 2004 (see table A.1).

The Canadian dollar appreciated substantially against the United States dollar in 2003 and 2004, but the negative impact on the economy has been offset by increases in the prices of oil and other commodities exported by Canada, as well as by strong external demand. As a result, corporate profits reached record highs, boosting business investment and employment growth, which, along with wage gains, supported consumer spending.

Business investment is being driven by strong growth in corporate profits

Inflation remains under control, despite the surge in oil prices and loose monetary conditions

Canada grows strongly, boosted by strong external demand and rising commodity prices

Figure IV.2.
Real short-term interest rates in the EU-12, Japan and the United States, January 1999-October 2004

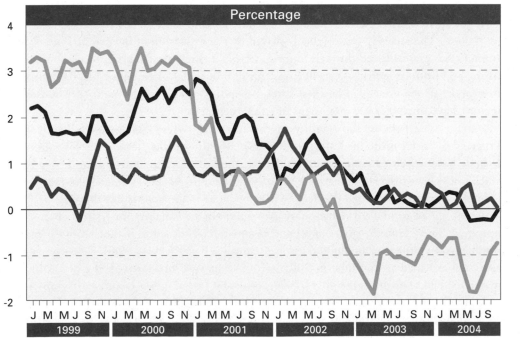

— EU-12
Japan
United States

Sources:
OECD, *Main Economic Indicators.*

However, with the further strengthening of the currency and the moderation in some commodity prices, the contribution to growth of net exports is expected to decline; some signs of weakening in exports had already become apparent in the last quarter of 2004. Meanwhile, since housing and automobile stocks have been built up considerably and interest rates are expected to rise over the next two years, it is unlikely that these two sectors will contribute to growth as they have in the past few years.

Government expenditure and public employment were weak in 2004, but stronger growth is expected in 2005. The fiscal position remains balanced, with federal surpluses offset to some extent by deficits at the provincial level. The federal government's budget surpluses are forecast to continue as the government adheres to its plan to reduce the ratio of public debt to GDP. Canada may be the only large developed country with both an ageing population and a sustainable fiscal position.

Interest rates in Canada are at least 70 basis points higher than those in the United States and are higher than the "equilibrium" differentials that might be expected in the light of Canada's lower long-term inflation, its fiscal position and its current-account balance. Monetary tightening in Canada is therefore expected to be less aggressive than in the United States in 2005.

Developed Asia and Pacific: recovery shifts to a lower gear

The economic recovery in Japan, which began in mid-2003, continues but has shifted to a lower gear, with signs of sluggishness since the second quarter of 2004. Nevertheless, GDP increased by 3.6 per cent for the year, the best annual performance in the past decade. Growth in 2005 is, however, expected to decelerate to 2 per cent (see table A.1). The prospects for the Japanese economy remain largely dependent on a number of external factors, including the strength of the United States and China, oil prices, and the global information and communication technologies (ICT) cycle; the appreciation of the yen vis-à-vis the United States dollar has not yet become a major curb on economic activity.

External demand
drives the recovery,
but domestic demand
is picking up strength

The recovery was originally driven by the expansion of the external sector, but strength has gradually fed through to other sectors, from manufacturing to non-manufacturing and from large firms to small firms. An improvement in corporate profits continues to support strong growth in business capital spending, while employment and household income have finally shown some signs of strengthening.

Financial system
risks are reduced

The risks to the stability of the financial system have subsided noticeably. Progress has been made in dealing with non-performing loans, conditions for corporate finance have improved, commercial banks continue to become more willing to lend and stock prices have been rising for more than a year; land prices, however, continue their prolonged downtrend, although the decline in a few metropolitan areas has slowed.

Deflationary forces
have been nearly
eliminated ...

The protracted deflationary trend has abated notably but has not been fully uprooted. The rise in the prices of oil and raw materials has led to higher producer prices, but consumer prices, excluding food prices, continue a slight downtrend. These cross currents are expected to continue in 2005, with the upward pressures on the prices of raw materials, and thus producer prices, being offset by restraints on labour costs and firms' lack of pricing power due to competitive pressures. Consumer prices are expected to register a small rise in late 2005, as the economic recovery gradually narrows the output gap, bringing the deflationary cycle to an end (see figure IV.3).

Figure IV.3.
**Inflation in the EU-12, Japan and the
United States, January 1999-October 2004**

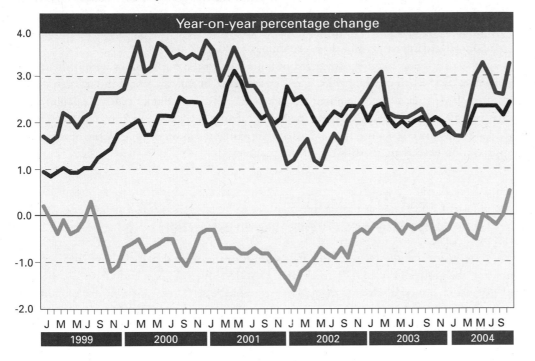

EU-12

Japan

United States

Sources:
OECD, *Main Economic
Indicators*, CPI for Japan and
United States, HICP for EU12.

Monetary policy has been accommodative, as the Bank of Japan has been increasing the monetary target to provide liquidity through various money market operations. The Bank has committed to maintain its zero-interest-rate policy until the annual changes in the CPI are above zero on a sustained basis; this is unlikely before late 2005.

On the other hand, fiscal policy will continue to be restrictive, mainly through expenditure restraint, such as cuts in public investment spending. Japan is aiming for a primary balance before 2010: raising the consumption tax could be an option in the medium term and privatization of the Postal Savings system is also on the agenda.

The downside risks in the short run include a further increase in oil prices, a "hard landing" in China and a downturn in the United States. Longer-term risks are more structural in nature. Corporate debt levels remain high, particularly for non-manufacturing firms, while progress in restoring the financial soundness of the banking system has been uneven. The government fiscal position remains precarious: the ratio of gross debt to GDP is 166 per cent, that of net debt to GDP is 80 per cent, and the structural deficit (including social security) is 6 per cent of GDP.

The economies of Australia and New Zealand performed well in 2004, with GDP growth of 3.4 per cent and 4 per cent, respectively; however, growth in both, particularly New Zealand, is expected to moderate in 2005 (see table A.1).

In Australia, a scaling back in housing construction, which has been the most vibrant force for economic growth for the previous few years, was offset by an improvement in the terms of trade (due to higher prices for its commodity exports) and a fiscal stimulus. In New Zealand, domestic demand has been booming, bolstered by business investment and housing construction. Both economies have achieved notable employment growth, to the point where unemployment rates have reached historical lows. Import

*... as monetary
policy remains
accommodative...*

*... while fiscal policy is
restrictive*

*Australia and New
Zealand grew
strongly in 2004,
but are expected
to moderate in 2005*

demand has been growing at more than 10 per cent in real terms in both economies, but real exports have also increased, although at a lower pace than imports. Both economies have external deficits of about 5 per cent of GDP. Australia reduced its deficit slightly in 2004 due to the higher value of its exports, but New Zealand's deficit deteriorated further. The external deficits and the appreciation of their currencies suggest that there may be some downward adjustment in these economies in 2005.

Inflation has moved upward in both economies, but remains within the target ranges set by the two central banks. The Reserve Bank of Australia held interest rates constant in 2004, after raising them in 2003, whereas the Reserve Bank of New Zealand raised rates by 150 basis points in 2004. No further tightening is expected in 2005, although New Zealand may reverse some of the earlier tightening if slower immigration or currency appreciation exacerbate the slowing of the economy.

Western Europe:
Can the recovery be sustained?

In Western Europe, the recovery lost momentum in the second half of 2004. In the third quarter, the growth of real GDP decelerated considerably; in France and Germany, the rate of expansion slowed almost to stagnation (see table A.2). There was also a weakening of cyclical growth in the United Kingdom of Great Britain and Northern Ireland, which is at a more advanced stage in its current business cycle. Business surveys point to moderate expansion in Western Europe in the final quarter of 2004. For the year as a whole, real GDP increased by some 2.3 per cent (see table I.1); the rise in oil prices, only partially offset by the appreciation of the euro, is estimated to have reduced growth by some 0.3 percentage points.

Net exports weaken and investment improves marginally, but private consumption remains sluggish

A major factor behind the deceleration in economic activity in the third quarter of 2004 was the weakening of export growth, which had been the mainstay of the recovery since the second half of 2003. At the same time, import demand remained strong. As a result, the contribution of real net exports to growth, which declined in the second quarter, turned negative. This was, however, largely offset by an acceleration in inventory investment and an upturn of fixed investment. In contrast, private consumption remained sluggish, held back by the rise in energy prices and a more uncertain outlook for jobs.

Against this background, short-term growth remains vulnerable to a further deterioration of the external environment. Real GDP in Western Europe as a whole is forecast to increase by 2¼ per cent in 2005, broadly the same as in the preceding year (see table I.1). The appreciation of the euro and other European currencies in late 2004 has raised concerns regarding price competitiveness and clouded the prospects for export growth, formerly the main pillar of the expected continuation of the recovery in 2005. In the euro area, the problem remains the weakness of domestic demand which does not have the underlying momentum necessary to offset an adverse export shock.

Domestic demand is expected to improve in 2005

Nevertheless, a moderate upturn in final domestic demand in the euro area is forecast for 2005. Business fixed investment should continue to strengthen, stimulated by favourable financing conditions, higher capacity utilization rates and a pent-up need for replacement and modernization of machinery and equipment. Private household consumption expenditures should be supported by gains in employment and associated increases in aggregate disposable incomes. Changes in real net exports will (as in 2004) make only a slightly positive contribution to growth.

Among the major economies, real GDP in Germany is forecast to increase by only 1½ per cent in 2005. Somewhat stronger growth is expected in France and Italy. In the United Kingdom, cyclical momentum will weaken in 2005 and growth will be more in line with trend output growth of 2¾ per cent. This is a desirable development in view of the little remaining slack in the economy, which could lead to upward pressures on inflation.

Germany remains the laggard

The employment response to the cyclical upturn in output was 0.5 per cent in 2004 compared with the preceding year (see figure IV.4). This reflected not only the moderate strength of the recovery but also the fact that labour hoarding in the downturn had prevented a decline in demand for labour. It also appears that the stimulus provided by the labour market reforms in a number of countries over the past decade, designed to increase part-time work and other flexible working arrangements, have started to fade. The unemployment rate remained broadly stable at about 8 per cent in 2004. Employment growth is forecast to strengthen moderately in 2005 and the average unemployment rate will fall slightly (see table A.1).

Employment creation remains weak, but some improvement is expected in 2005

Consumer price inflation (as measured by the Harmonized Index of Consumer Prices (HICP)) averaged somewhat more than 2 per cent in the euro area in 2004. The impact of the surge in oil prices was largely limited to upward pressures on final energy prices, which led to a temporary increase in inflation to 2.4 per cent in October 2004. Core inflation was close to 2 per cent during the first ten months of the year. Headline inflation is forecast to fall during 2005 to below the ceiling of 2 per cent established by the European Central Bank (ECB) (see table A.1). The uncertain outlook for jobs suggests that a wage-price spiral resulting from the second-round effects of higher oil prices in the labour market are small.

Oil prices boost headline inflation, but underlying inflationary pressures are contained

Figure IV.4.
Unemployment rates in the EU-15, Japan and the United States, January 1999-October 2004

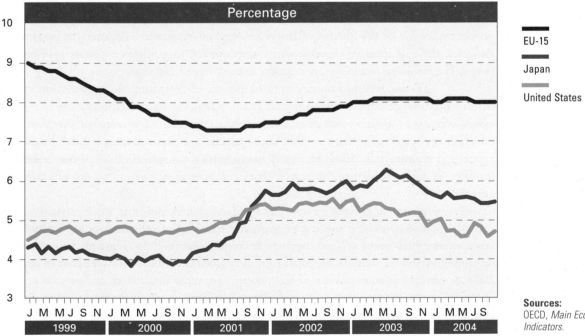

EU-15

Japan

United States

Sources:
OECD, *Main Economic Indicators.*

Fiscal policy, as gauged by changes in the cyclically adjusted primary balance (which excludes interest payments), was supportive of economic activity in the euro area in 2004, but is projected to become slightly restrictive in 2005. Outside the euro area, fiscal policy in the United Kingdom shifted to a slightly restrictive stance in 2004, following strong increases in government spending from 2001 to 2003. The timing of government spending programmes was an important factor behind the resilience of the United Kingdom economy to the global economic downturn after 2000.

The average general government budget deficit in the euro area was equivalent to 2.9 per cent of GDP in 2004. Budget deficits remained significantly above the Stability and Growth Pact (SGP) threshold of 3 per cent in France and Germany for the third consecutive year. In Greece, a shortfall of net revenues from the Olympic Games contributed to a budget deficit of more than 5 per cent of GDP in 2004, and revised data showed that deficits had also been above the 3 per cent ceiling in 2000-2003.

In late summer 2004, the European Commission made proposals aiming to increase the flexibility of the Stability and Growth Pact:[1] The current ceilings of 3 per cent and 60 per cent for deficit and debt to GDP ratios, respectively, would be maintained, but the focus would be shifted to debt and sustainability, rather than the current emphasis on deficits. More account would be taken of different economic and debt situations, so that countries with low levels of debt and sound finances could have more flexibility; there would be more emphasis on pre-emptive action to correct inadequate budgetary developments, particularly during good times, through early warnings and peer pressure; the "exceptional circumstances" clause, under which a country may run a deficit above the ceiling of 3 per cent if it has a negative rate of growth of 2 per cent or more, would be broadened to include a situation of protracted slowdown; and a more flexible path for the correction of excessive deficits would be allowed to take into account country-specific economic developments and to minimize the necessity of pro-cyclical adjustments. A consensus among governments on these matters may not be easy to achieve.

Monetary policy stances in the euro area and the United Kingdom diverged in 2004, reflecting different stages in the business cycle and related differential concerns about inflationary risks. In the euro area, the ECB's main financing rate has been unchanged at 2 per cent since June 2003 because of fragile growth and moderate inflationary expectations. However, the real effective appreciation of the euro led to a further tightening of overall monetary conditions in the euro area in the second half of 2004.

The weakening recovery in third quarter of 2004 and the appreciation of the euro in the final months of the year have led to a revision of expectations that the ECB would start to raise interest rates in the first quarter of 2005. In view of the increased uncertainty regarding growth, together with expectations that inflation will fall below the 2 per cent threshold in 2005, the ECB can maintain its wait-and-see policy until the recovery is well established; this will require a sustained strengthening of domestic demand.

In contrast, robust growth, tight labour markets and little spare capacity in the United Kingdom economy led to a progressive tightening of monetary policy in 2004 to avoid an overshooting of the government's inflation target in 2005. The policy interest rate was raised in several steps from 3.5 per cent in November 2003 to 4.75 per cent in August 2004. A further tightening of monetary policy is expected in 2005 to ensure that output grows in line with potential. Increased risks of inflation also prompted a tightening of monetary policy in Switzerland in 2004.

The expectation of a continued recovery in Western Europe depends heavily on further robust growth in the global economy and the associated import demand from the rest of the world. The recovery is therefore vulnerable to a possible deterioration in the external environment: an unexpected weakening of global growth, not necessarily related only to oil market developments, could cause the recovery to falter. For example, further appreciation of the euro could act as a brake on economic growth in Western Europe. In some countries (Ireland, Spain and the United Kingdom), there are also risks of a possible reversal of the rise in house prices, with negative wealth effects and adverse repercussions on private household consumption and overall economic growth.

Oil prices, global demand, exchange rates and house prices pose risks for 2005

The new European Union members—a strong rebound

Economic activity in the eight new European Union (EU) member States from Central and Eastern Europe (EU-8) picked up noticeably in 2004. Their aggregate GDP expanded by some 5 per cent, led by the export-driven recovery in Poland. All Baltic economies continued to grow at a brisk pace. However, the peak of the current cycle was probably reached in mid-2004 (see figure IV.5) and the pace of expansion is likely to decelerate in the short run.

Broad-based expansion follows EU accession

In 2004, growth in the EU-8 economies became more broadly based, driven by robust consumption and investment expenditure and strengthening external demand. Net exports continued to make a positive contribution to GDP growth in Poland and Slovakia, but their impact remained negative elsewhere because strong domestic demand resulted in

Figure IV.5.
Growth of GDP and industrial output in Central Europe and the Baltic States (EU-8), quarterly, 2000-2004

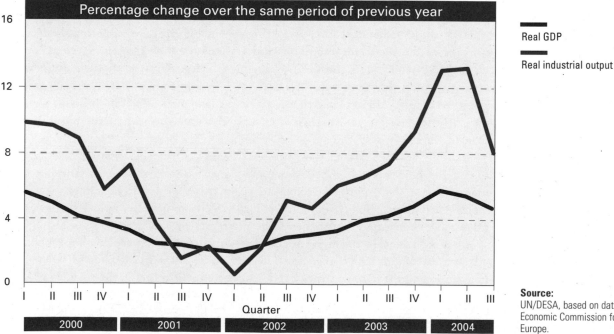

Real GDP

Real industrial output

Source:
UN/DESA, based on data of Economic Commission for Europe.

vigorous import growth. At the same time, export performance generally improved, reflecting the impact of virtually full trade liberalization (particularly the abolition of quotas for food products) between the new EU members and the EU-15, the improved quality of products and increased participation in international distribution networks. This robust export performance is expected to continue in 2005, reinforced by the positive effect of new foreign direct investment (FDI) inflows. Improved corporate profits, stronger business confidence and expectations of lower corporate taxes, as well as the implementation of EU-related projects, also contributed to an upturn in investment in 2004; this is expected to continue in 2005.

The outlook for 2005 is encouraging

Although output growth has started to decelerate, economic sentiment indicators suggest a favourable short-term outlook for the EU-8 area. The average rate of GDP growth in the region will remain around 4 per cent in 2005, despite some slowdown attributable to lower export growth (see table A.1). An increase in greenfield FDI projects should accelerate the ongoing restructuring and boost productive capacity.

Employment still has to pick-up

In 2004, the labour market improved only marginally, with the exception of Slovakia. Despite the acceleration of output growth, net job creation was weak, although unemployment declined slightly. There is a duality in the labour market in that skilled-labour bottlenecks coexist with an absence of vacancies for the low-skilled jobseekers that dominate the pool of long-term unemployed. In the short run, job creation is likely to remain weak and even the output growth anticipated for 2005 is likely to result in only modest employment gains.

EU accession drives up consumer prices

Inflation increased in the EU-8 countries in 2004, largely reflecting one-off factors related to the EU accession, such as VAT unification and price deregulation, but also the rising prices of imported energy and stronger export demand. Since most of the price deregulation has been completed and real wage growth has slowed, inflation is likely to subside in 2005 in the region as a whole.

Macroeconomic policies remain mixed

Macroeconomic policies were broadly supportive of growth in 2004. Good fiscal outcomes allowed the central banks to preserve their accommodative monetary policies, although some monetary tightening took place in the Czech Republic, Latvia and Poland in response to higher inflation and strong credit expansion. Fiscal deficits either declined or stagnated throughout the EU-8 area, with the notable exception of Poland. Budget outturns exceeded expectations (except for Hungary) as a result of strong tax revenues, reflecting higher-than-expected growth. The structural components of the deficits, however, remained almost the same, with subsidies to loss-making enterprises and state loan guarantees continuing. Modest fiscal consolidation is planned for 2005, in line with a gradual movement towards the euro zone entry criteria. However, this is to be combined with co-financing of EU assistance.

Stagnation in the EU-15 and populist domestic policies pose risks

The main external downside risks to the outlook include a possible deceleration of economic growth in the euro zone and higher-than-expected energy prices. A major internal risk is the danger of election-driven increases in public spending; these could undermine policy credibility and would probably result in monetary tightening, lower FDI inflows and reduced competitiveness. The most pressing policy challenges facing these countries are the achievement of sustainable fiscal consolidation and the implementation of structural reforms for job-rich growth. Other policy challenges include EU-related harmonization and the improvement of agricultural competitiveness in the enlarged EU.

Economies in transition

Southern and Eastern Europe— retaining growth momentum

Economic activity in Southern and Eastern Europe strengthened in 2004 (see figure IV.6). For the year as a whole, aggregate GDP rose by almost 7 per cent on the strength of output in the region's largest economy—Romania. The broad-based recovery in Bulgaria also gained further ground while GDP in Serbia and Montenegro surged after the poor outcome in 2003. Economic expansion in the remaining parts of the region was more moderate. Intraregional trade in the region increased, following a number of bilateral trade agreements (BTAs). Output in the large agricultural sectors of all Southern and Eastern European economies was boosted by good harvests. In 2004, strong domestic demand, bolstered by strong credit growth, continued to support economic activity in Bulgaria and Romania, but in Croatia the problem of twin deficits and a rapidly growing foreign debt prompted restrictive policy measures. The EU candidate countries (Bulgaria, Croatia and Romania) continue to benefit from a surge in inward FDI; this has contributed to a deepening of the restructuring, the modernization of their economies and an acceleration of export growth.

Growth of output and trade strengthens

Most Southern and Eastern European economies are expected to preserve a strong growth momentum in 2005 but, compared to 2004, the average rate of GDP growth in the region is likely to slow. Overall, domestic demand is set to remain buoyant and should provide support to economic activity in the region.

Outlook for growth remains optimistic

Figure IV.6.
Growth of GDP and industrial output in Southern and Eastern Europe, quarterly, 2000-2004

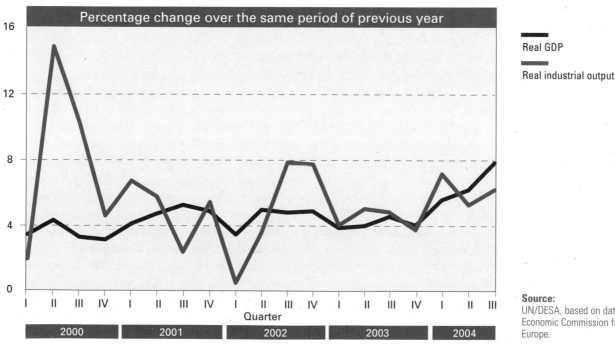

Real GDP

Real industrial output

Source:
UN/DESA, based on data of Economic Commission for Europe.

In 2004, employment increased in Bulgaria but remained stagnant in Croatia and declined in Romania. The concomitant decline in unemployment rates in Croatia and Romania suggests withdrawals from the labour force. The situation in the labour markets of the remaining countries generally deteriorated in 2004, with some countries facing excessively high unemployment rates. Given the ongoing enterprise restructuring in the region, no major improvements can be expected in 2005. Demand may pick up only for certain categories of labour, driven by expanding business activity.

Consumer price
inflation slowed

Disinflation continued in most countries in 2004, reflecting relatively tight fiscal policies and, in some cases, nominal effective exchange-rate appreciation. In contrast, producer price inflation generally accelerated, to a large extent as a result of higher energy prices. These price increases will likely be passed on to consumers in 2005, suggesting a reversal in the disinflation trend; however, this should not result in a resurgence of high inflation.

Macroeconomic policy in most countries remained restrictive in 2004. In line with rising incomes and, in some cases, the expansion of credit, monetary policy is likely to stay restrictive. To curb domestic demand, there is likely to be a further tightening of the fiscal stance and additional measures to restrict credit growth, such as more restrictive prudential banking regulations.

Current-account
deficits and imported
inflation threaten
price stability

Most Southern and Eastern European economies have current-account deficits that increased as a result of higher energy prices in 2004. The risks to the outlook for these countries are associated with possible negative external shocks, such as protracted sluggishness in Western European import demand. In addition, if imported inflation continues to rise, this may prompt a more restrictive policy stance.

Commonwealth of Independent States: is the boom fading?

Strong growth
continues for a second
consecutive year, but
will moderate in 2005

Very strong growth continued in the Commonwealth of Independent States (CIS) for a second consecutive year, with GDP increasing by over 7 per cent (see table A.3). The whole CIS region, including the largest economy, the Russian Federation, continued to benefit from the surge in world commodity prices. Growth is set to moderate gradually in 2005 but will remain robust, with aggregate GDP increasing by about 6 per cent.

In most resource-rich CIS economies, the main factor behind the robust output growth remained the rapid expansion of commodity exports, in particular oil and natural gas. At the same time, several years of continuing strong output recovery have been associated with a surge in domestic demand, especially private consumption. In many countries, fixed investment has also rebounded, with the bulk being directed towards the extractive industries. With imports outpacing exports in most CIS economies (Ukraine being a notable exception), real net exports in general contributed negatively to GDP growth in 2004.

GDP and industrial
output are losing
momentum

After some deceleration in the pace of economic activity in the second half of 2004, growth in the region as a whole is expected to lose further momentum in 2005. This is reflected in the downturn in the growth of both GDP and industrial output (see figure IV.7), which suggests that the current boom may be fading. This same pattern of decelerating growth is expected to prevail in all large CIS economies—the Russian Federation,

Figure IV.7.
Growth of GDP and industrial output in the Commonwealth of Independent States, quarterly, 2000-2004

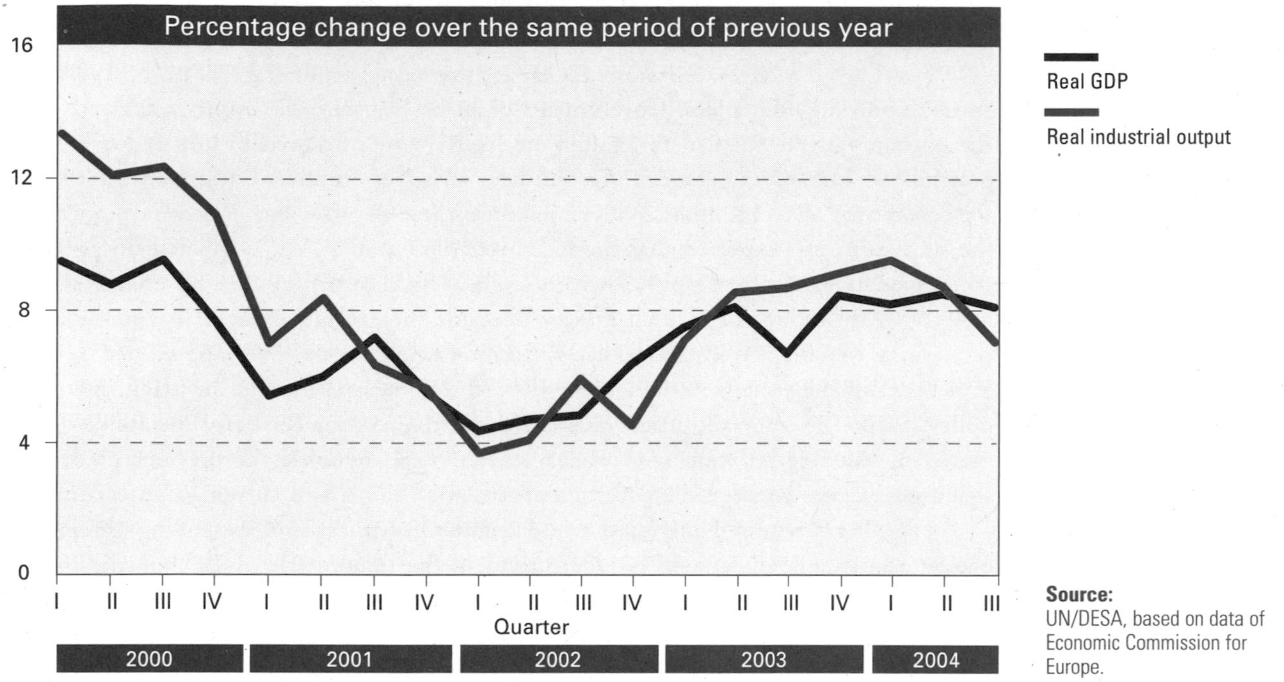
Percentage change over the same period of previous year
16
12
8
4
0
I II III IV I II III IV I II III IV I II III IV I II III
Quarter
2000
2001
2002
2003
2004
Real GDP
Real industrial output

Source: UN/DESA, based on data of Economic Commission for Europe.

Ukraine, Belarus and Kazakhstan—as a result of external developments, namely less vigorous commodity prices and weaker demand in the region's main markets. Domestic demand in the CIS is expected to remain generally buoyant but its effect on national economies will depend on the supply responsiveness of domestic producers.

Labour markets are still lagging behind the adjustment in output

Towards the end of 2004, the number of involuntarily unemployed in the CIS averaged some 10 million, some 8 per cent of the economically active population. Total employment has continued to increase since the last quarter of 2003, but this trend mainly reflects developments in some of the largest economies, such as the Russian Federation and Kazakhshtan. There may be some further improvements in labour markets in the short run, but labour adjustment has in general been lagging the adjustment in output because many CIS economies have not yet completed their restructuring.

Disinflation is likely to be reversed in some countries in the short run

The moderate disinflation in the region as a whole in 2004 involved marked variations across countries. Food prices, which have a large weight in consumer baskets, rose less rapidly than in 2003, but stronger producer price inflation in mid-2004 is feeding through to consumer prices in many countries, increasing inflationary expectations. Moreover, cost pressures have intensified, with labour costs rising faster than producer prices. The recovery in consumer demand is likely to fuel further inflationary pressure. Supply-side problems, such as the closure of major refineries in Ukraine or a bad harvest, are also causing an acceleration of inflation rates in some countries. As a result, the disinflationary trend may be reversed in some countries of the region in the short run.

Despite rapid growth, macroeconomic policy in many CIS economies has been expansionary in recent years. The pro-cyclical bias in public spending became apparent in some countries in 2004 and resulted in a deterioration of their structural fiscal balances. At the same time, the currencies of most commodity-exporting economies were under growing upward pressure because of surging export revenues.

With their Stabilization Funds accumulating windfall gains from export revenues due to high oil prices, Governments of such resource-rich countries as Azerbaijan, Kazakhstan and the Russian Federation are likely to be pressured to pursue looser fiscal policies over the forecast period; this will have an adverse impact on inflation. However, the capacity of macroeconomic policy to address these negative implications is limited. In the short run, it is expected that the macroeconomic policy stance will remain generally accommodative, with a risk of further pro-cyclical fiscal loosening in some countries.

Symptoms of "Dutch Disease" became increasingly evident in 2004 in some economies, in particular in the Russian Federation where the currency appreciated by some 5 per cent in the year. Nevertheless, in view of the persistently high inflation, monetary policy in 2005 in some countries, such as Kazakhstan and the Russian Federation, will be geared to reducing inflation as a primary objective, abandoning the previous practice of striking a balance between the government's inflation target and currency appreciation.

As a result of increased world commodity prices and expanding volumes of energy exports, the merchandise trade surplus of the resource-rich CIS countries rose in 2004, but is expected to moderate as imports of consumer and investment goods pick up in 2005. Some other countries of the region, such as Ukraine, have current-account surpluses largely as the result of high net transfers and net receipts for services. Countries with rising imports and current-account deficits have not faced difficulties because foreign direct investment has remained a major source of finance.

The main weakness of the CIS economies remains their high dependence on exports of natural resources and low value-added products, which makes them highly vulnerable to external shocks. The current expansion of commodity exports seems unlikely to be sustainable, with the result that the main source of the recent high economic growth may dissipate in the not-too-distant future. The long-term growth prospects of the CIS economies therefore hinge on their success in economic diversification, as well as further improvements in domestic product and financial markets.

Developing countries

Africa

Africa achieved its highest growth in almost a decade in 2004, with real GDP estimated to have grown by 4.5 per cent (see figure IV.8). This improvement over 4 per cent in 2003 was underpinned by the global recovery, higher commodity prices, increased oil production and prices, good macroeconomic management, better performance in agriculture, an improved political situation in many countries and continued donor support in the form of aid and debt relief. Industrial expansion, particularly in construction and mining, growth in the tourism sector and rising FDI contributed to the region's higher growth.

Africa is expected to grow at 4¾ per cent in 2005, driven by the favourable growth prospects for the majority of countries in the region. Continued good macroeconomic fundamentals, a global environment that will boost Africa's exports, better per-

Figure IV.8.
Real GDP growth in Africa, 2003-2005

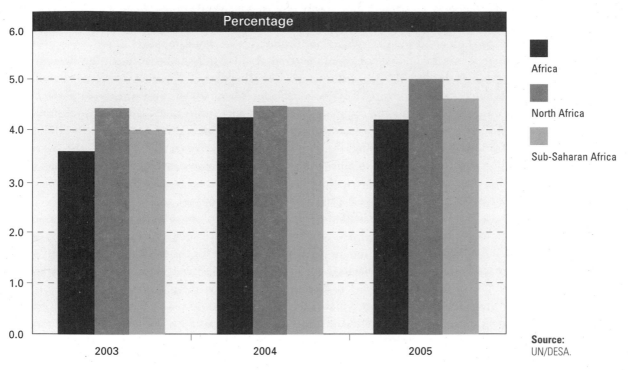

formance in the agricultural sector (assuming continued good weather conditions) and growth in the services, tourism and mining sectors are expected to be the primary factors driving this growth.

Despite its improved performance, Africa falls short of the 7 per cent growth considered necessary to meet the principal Millennium Development Goal of halving poverty by 2015. Only six countries—Angola, Chad, Equatorial Guinea, Ethiopia, Liberia and Mozambique—grew by more than 7 per cent in 2004; only Chad, Equatorial Guinea and Mozambique have sustained growth in excess of 7 per cent since 2001, and Angola since 2002. With the exception of Mozambique, growth in these countries is driven largely by the oil sector. As the oil sector is capital intensive, its direct contribution to poverty reduction through employment generation is limited while its limited backward and forward linkages with the rest of the economy may mean that high growth does not translate into meaningful poverty reduction.

The GDP growth of the five largest African economics (Algeria, Egypt, Morocco, Nigeria and South Africa) is forecast to improve from 3.9 per cent in 2004 to over 4 per cent in 2005. Growth in Algeria is expected to be above 6 per cent in 2004-2005 due to high oil and gas production and increased public expenditures. Egypt achieved growth of 3.2 per cent in 2004 as a result of an expansionary fiscal stance, buoyant export demand for its manufacturing and energy products and strong growth in tourism revenues. The proposed reduction of personal and corporate tax rates is expected to boost private consumption and investment, leading to higher growth in 2005. Morocco's GDP growth dropped to 4.2 per cent in 2004 from 5.2 per cent in 2003 because of a deceleration in the high growth in the agricultural sector, but a free trade agreement with the United States,

... but growth remains inadequate for a meaningful impact on poverty

Performance of the largest economies was mixed

signed in July 2004, is expected to mobilize more investment and increase the country's growth prospects in the near-term. Nigeria's growth slowed to 4.0 per cent in 2004 from 10.2 per cent in 2003, despite steady growth in the agricultural, manufacturing and services sectors. The deceleration in growth was caused mainly by civil unrest and the slow expansion of oil and gas production. Economy-wide work stoppages to protest against the increases in fuel prices caused by the removal of subsidies, a key element in Nigeria's economic reforms, also contributed to the slowdown. Nigeria's National Economic Empowerment Strategy (NEEDS), launched in March 2004, constitutes an important step towards confronting the country's macroeconomic, institutional and structural problems while securing strong economic growth and poverty eradication. South Africa's GDP grew by 3 per cent in 2004 owing largely to strong domestic demand generated by the low inflation and interest rate environment and by higher disposable incomes as a result of tax relief measures. Increased export revenues also contributed to South Africa's GDP growth in 2004. The same factors are expected to continue to support growth in 2005.

The number of countries suffering economic contraction declined in 2004

Only Côte d'Ivoire, Seychelles and Zimbabwe suffered economic contraction in 2004, compared to seven countries in 2003. Political crises, armed clashes and other civil disturbances took a toll on the Ivorian economy for the third consecutive year, while macroeconomic fundamentals were behind Seychelles' continued poor performance in 2004. Zimbabwe's economy has been contracting for the past five years; the poor performance in 2004 was attributable to droughts that affected agricultural output, lack of coherent economic policy and the ongoing political crisis.

Macroeconomic policies remain sound

Africa continued to improve macroeconomic conditions in 2004. On average, monetary and fiscal policies have been relatively tight in recent years. Inflation has been under control, with most countries maintaining single- or low double-digit rates of consumer price inflation. In 2004, the pressure from increased oil prices was offset by good harvests and lower prices for staple foods. In many parts of the continent, especially in Communauté financière africaine (CFA) countries and South Africa, currency appreciation slowed imported inflation (particularly from higher fuel prices) and its transmission to domestic prices. Central government fiscal deficits are estimated to have fallen from an average of 1.5 per cent of GDP in 2003 to 0.8 per cent in 2004, despite the increased spending for poverty reduction in many countries. This was made possible by foreign grants and successful revenue-enhancement schemes, mainly improved tax collection, in some countries. Monetary policy tightening is expected in many countries in order to manage inflationary pressures if the higher oil prices persist. Overall, it is expected that the region will continue to pursue prudent monetary, fiscal and exchange rate policies in 2005.

Debt relief is extended to some additional countries

Continued debt relief and strong export earnings contributed to the alleviation of the public sector external debt burden in 2004. Five African countries—Ethiopia, Ghana, Madagascar, Niger and Senegal—reached the completion point of the enhanced HIPC programme and received further debt relief in 2004. Burundi and the Republic of the Congo are expected to reach the decision point in 2005.

The region achieves a surplus on its current account

Following deficits for three consecutive years, Africa achieved a current-account surplus of 1.2 per cent of GDP in 2004. To a large extent, this was due to rising oil and commodity prices. The number of countries with a surplus on the current account increased from 11 in 2003 to 14 in 2004, of which eight are oil producers. In 2004, the region also benefited from increases in non-oil commodity prices that, to a large degree, were driven by strong demand from Asia (see chapter II). Prices of all of Africa's key non-oil export commodities increased, except for cocoa, Robusta coffee and groundnut oil, for which prices declined in 2004, due largely to increases in world production.

There are several downside risks to economic growth on the continent in 2005. Any adjustment to the large current-account deficit of the United States that reduces growth in the global economy would have negative consequences for Africa. Moreover, the United States current-account deficit has spurred protectionist sentiments in that country. At a time when a number of African countries are beginning to establish a foothold in non-commodity world markets, new protectionist measures that affect the region would seriously damage prospects. The uncertainty regarding oil prices poses differentiated risks to the region since it encompasses both oil-exporting and oil-importing countries. Regionally, contagion from the political instability in Côte d'Ivoire, the Sudan and Zimbabwe may affect neighbouring countries and overall growth prospects for Africa. Finally, the forecasts for African growth depend on projections of normal agricultural production. The good weather in the planting phases of the 2004/2005 crop cycles in several countries give cause for optimism in this respect, but Africa's vulnerability to adverse weather conditions could influence agricultural production and cloud the outlook for 2005.

The region faces a variety of downside risks

Western Asia: windfall oil revenue reinvigorates economic activity

In 2004, increased oil production, together with soaring oil prices, boosted economic growth in Western Asia to 5.5 per cent, improved both fiscal and external balances, expanded intraregional trade and invigorated capital flows within the region. With GDP growth of about 4.5 per cent, the oil-exporting countries of the region maintained their economic upswing that started in 2003 (see figure IV.9).

Figure IV.9.
GDP per capita for Western Asia, 2001-2004

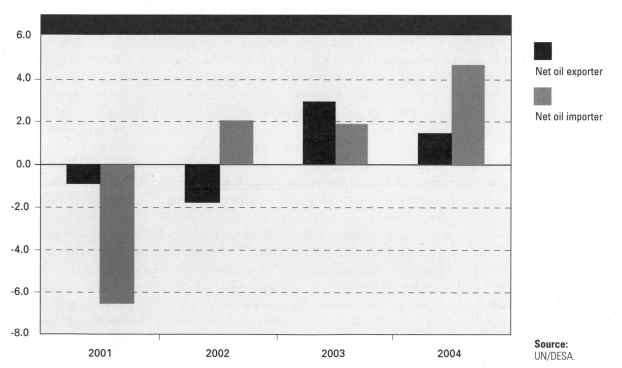

Net oil exporter

Net oil importer

Source:
UN/DESA.

Windfall oil revenues
also benefited the oil-
importing countries
of the region

For their part, growth in the oil-importing countries accelerated to 6.7 per cent in 2004—the highest since 1990. Among other factors, these countries were buoyed by the spillover effects of rising incomes in the oil-exporting countries through such channels as workers' remittances, financial flows, and intraregional trade and tourism. On the other hand, some of these countries are still confronted with the loss of either the Iraqi export market (mainly Jordan, Lebanon and Yemen), subsidized oil imports from Iraq (Jordan) or transit-trade revenues (the oil pipeline through the Syrian Arab Republic). Encouragingly, however, the experience of 2004 indicates not only that the "oil shock" was absorbed in such oil-importing countries as Jordan but, more importantly, that opportunities for exports expanded and economic growth increased. Jordan's industrial, construction, trade, transport and tourism sectors led growth in 2004 and are expected to expand further during 2005. With their higher energy import bill, rising real GDP in these countries will come largely from the more cost-conscious private sector. Public revenue and expenditure will, on the other hand, be affected by uncertainty regarding oil import arrangements. In Lebanon, for example, the rising energy import bill is already causing increased interruptions in domestic electricity supplies which, in turn, affect output and economic growth.

Growth in Turkey reached about 12 per cent during the first half of 2004 and averaged 9 per cent for the year as whole. The expansion was driven by rising private spending, both consumption and investment. Continued monetary easing, credit expansion and currency appreciation contributed to the higher spending. Growth is expected to decelerate to around 6 per cent in 2005. In the case of Israel, exports of goods and services, mainly by high-tech industries benefiting from growth in the United States, led the expansion in 2004. Private investment rose in response to this export buoyancy and Government spending also increased, due mostly to security-related expenditures. As a result, GDP grew by about 3.6 per cent in 2004 (following 1.3 per cent in 2003), and growth is expected to remain around 3¾ per cent in 2005.

Oil revenue is
expected to reach
$220 billion in 2005

Although regional oil production and prices are expected to decline (see chapter II), the region's economic outlook remains favourable, with GDP growth expected to be around 4½ per cent in 2005. Total oil revenues in 2005 are expected to reach almost $220 billion, of which the six Gulf oil-exporting countries will receive some $190 billion and the remaining three oil exporters some $28 billion (Iraq around $20 billion, Yemen over $5 billion and the Syrian Arab Republic over $3 billion). Those high revenues will continue to fuel an economic boom in recipient countries although the situation in Iraq will remain difficult as long as political and security problems persist and the overhang of its external debt and reparations limit the availability of financing for reconstruction.[2]

Regional tourism
is rebounding

Intraregional tourism, already enjoying a recovery from the setbacks following 11 September 2001, accelerated its growth and positively affected the level of regional economic activity in 2004, particularly in Jordan, Lebanon and the Syrian Arab Republic. The number of tourists from the region is expected to continue rising in 2005, on the one hand because regional incomes have been positively affected by buoyant oil prices and, on the other, because of the relaxation of travel and visa requirements for Iraqi travelers.

Lagged wealth effects
will boost growth
in 2005

The upswing in the region is expected to continue in 2005 if relative political stability is maintained and as long as oil prices remain relatively buoyant. The "wealth effect" of increased oil revenue will increase expenditures of both Governments and the private sector and will be a positive influence in 2005. There is expected to be a lagged expenditure effect as the rising public revenues received by the oil-exporting economies during 2004 are used to increase public investment and other public expenditures in 2005. The effect of rising public expenditure is expected to spill over into domestic private incomes and the rising prosperity of households will, in turn, raise expenditures on goods, services and labour. The extent of the upturn will therefore be influenced by the volume of the lagged public expenditure, which will propel consumption and hence investment. The private sector in these countries will also have greater liquidity, especially in the largest regional economy, Saudi Arabia, where the Government has announced its intention to repay some of its large debt. Such repayments will reduce the interest differential between domestic credit and dollar credit, although interest rates will generally follow United States rates upwards.

The reversal of the "11 September effect" has also had an impact on capital flows, with some regional capital previously invested elsewhere returning to its home region. Regional stock markets and real estate prices boomed during 2003-2004. The liberalization of capital markets and of regulatory restrictions on real estate investment in Bahrain, Jordan, Lebanon and the Emirate of Dubai in the United Arab Emirates has spurred intraregional real estate investment flows, raising asset values and owners' perception of wealth. This personal "wealth effect" is currently contributing to a greater propensity to invest and spend locally and regionally. In 2005, the increased liquidity in Saudi Arabia will continue to fuel the region's financial markets and real estate boom. Similarly, rising liquidity in Kuwait, the United Arab Emirates and Qatar, among other countries, will inject additional financial resources into regional banking as well as recycle savings into major world financial centres.

2004 witnessed mildly rising rates of inflation, except in Iraq, the Occupied Palestinian Territory, Saudi Arabia and Yemen. This was attributed to the depreciation of the dollar against major world currencies on the one hand and to the filtering of increased nominal incomes and government expenditure into aggregate demand on the other. This duality of underlying causes in the inflationary process will accelerate in 2005 if the dollar continues its downward course and the import prices of foodstuffs and raw materials increase further. In addition, the increase in public expenditures will reinforce inflationary pressures.

Inflation is on the rise, reflecting dollar depreciation and the gradual removal of subsidies

The expected increase in aggregate demand in 2005 will enhance regional employment prospects while the spillover effects of United States military and civilian expenditure in Iraq and increasing reconstruction needs will continue spurring demand for contractual and subcontracting services, particularly from Kuwait and Jordan. However, due to the high stock of unemployed, especially among the youth, and the propensity of contractors and the private sector to employ non-nationals, it is unlikely that the high rates of regional unemployment will be pared. Despite policies to foster "Bahrainization", "Saudization" and "Omanization", private enterprise in the oil-exporting economies will probably continue to prefer employing lower-cost expatriates rather than nationals (for whom employers bear pension and other social costs). While some policies to increase the employment of nationals will induce labour substitution and create greater space for national labour in the oil-exporting countries, there will be some spillovers onto the broader labour market so that the size of the total labour force (national and non-national) will continue to grow in 2005. Unemployment rates will remain high in all countries of the region except those with low domestic labour contributions and those, such as the United Arab Emirates and Qatar, that have abundant public resources to absorb the unemployed. The non-regional component of the labour force will be affected by both demographic and immigration pressures and, with the spread of female education over time, the increasing entry of female nationals into the labour market. Within the oil-importing subregion, the unemployment rates in Jordan (officially 14.5 per cent in 2003), Lebanon, the Occupied

Despite the improved economic outlook, unemployment is unlikely to fall in 2005

Palestinian Territory (28.6 per cent in 2004), and Yemen (11.0 per cent in 2004) will not be easily dented, especially as labour supply growth rates also tend to be high.

Financial leakages abroad through extraregional workers' remittances, through the recycling of savings from the region and through increased demand for imported goods and services will reduce the regional multiplier effect. On the other hand, they will raise demand elsewhere: the region's economic boom will also be transmitted to countries outside Western Asia, mainly through two main channels. First, there will greater demand for migrant workers and increased flows of workers' remittances, mostly to South Asia and the Philippines, which are the countries of origin of many of Western Asia's lower-skilled workers. In addition, the boom will have a spillover effect through rising imports, many of which originate in Japan and the EU.

South Asia: resilience despite slowdown

Regional economic growth in 2004 is estimated at 6.3 per cent, falling 0.4 percentage points short of growth in the previous year. In 2003, exceptionally good weather resulted in a strong agricultural performance whereas growth in 2004 was undermined by less favourable weather conditions, with below normal rainfalls in Sri Lanka, India and Pakistan and heavy floods in Bangladesh.

The services and manufacturing sectors were the main drivers of growth for the net oil-importing countries in 2004, a trend which is expected to continue in 2005. Higher oil and non-oil commodity prices began to weigh on the net oil-importing countries of the region, while the Islamic Republic of Iran benefited from the higher oil prices, as well as from increased oil production and exports. In 2005, normal weather conditions should allow for a rebound in agricultural production. Some slowdown in the global economy is expected to reduce external demand for the region's main exports, but a slight decline in oil prices will benefit net oil importers, while slowing Iran's growth performance only marginally.

A number of South and East Asian countries suffered a severe blow when they were hit by tsunamis on 26 December 2004. The immediate human toll is unprecedented but a full assessment of the damage to infrastructure and other physical capital will not be possible until later in 2005. The international community committed over $5 billion in assistance in the month following the disaster but reconstruction will require a continued international response if long-term development prospects are to be restored. In the short term, however, a major impact on the economic growth of the affected countries is not expected since the damage to industrial and port facilities was limited and offshore oil and gas fields were spared. Extensive economic disruption is therefore expected only in the tourism sector and will be particularly acute in Sri Lanka and Thailand, where tourism accounts for around 6 per cent and 2 per cent of GDP, respectively. The tragedy has reduced the forecasts of growth for these two countries in 2005 by about one quarter to one percentage point, but growth rates in other countries will most likely not be affected, as reconstruction activities financed by government spending and international aid inflows will at least partially offset other losses. Even with these adjustments, regional GDP growth is forecast to remain around 6¼ per cent (see table A.5) in 2005.

There was particularly strong growth of large-scale manufacturing in Pakistan in 2004 (driven mainly by strong textile export growth), and industrial production also registered healthy growth in India and Bangladesh due to strong domestic and external demand.

Services growth was even stronger than manufacturing growth in India owing to its fast growing information technology (IT) and IT-related business-services sectors. In Sri Lanka, services growth was driven particularly by telecommunications, transport and tourism. Meanwhile, after some recovery in 2003 and 2004, tourist arrivals in Nepal started to decline again in September (on a year-on-year basis). Given the unstable security situation, this downward trend is likely to continue well into 2005, and economic performance in Nepal will continue to rely heavily on aid inflows and workers' remittances.

The region's international trade was buoyant in 2004 and is expected to remain strong in 2005, although export growth will slow from its performance in 2004 due to weakening external demand growth (see chapter II). The phasing out of the Agreement on Textiles and Clothing (ATC) at the beginning of 2005 is expected to at least initially hurt Bangladesh's and Sri Lanka's exports of readymade garments, while benefiting India and Pakistan.

A slowdown in export growth is expected for 2005 ...

Except for the Sri Lankan rupee and the Iranian rial, regional currencies remained broadly stable against the dollar in 2004. The Indian rupee appreciated for the second consecutive year, in spite of a steep depreciation following the national elections in April. With the new Government broadly following the economic reform course of its predecessor, markets recovered and foreign capital inflows picked up again, strengthening the rupee and bolstering reserves. By year-end, foreign exchange reserves had increased throughout the region, with the exception of Sri Lanka, where they fell due to central bank intervention to stem the depreciation of the rupee. For 2005, widening trade deficits in most countries and persistent inflation differentials suggest a gradual depreciation of regional currencies against the dollar, except for the Indian rupee, which will appreciate further due to continuing strong capital inflows.

... but stable currencies and ample reserves highlight the region's new external strength

Inflationary pressures picked up throughout the region, driven by high oil and non-oil commodity prices, as well as food prices (see figure IV.10). Only Nepal and Iran witnessed a fall in average inflation in 2004. In the latter case, this was a result of the petering out of the inflationary pressures stemming from the unification of the foreign exchange rate in 2002; even so, double-digit inflation persists.

Inflation is picking up, and the cycle of monetary easing has ended

In most countries, wholesale prices started rising in mid-2004, but the feed-through of higher oil prices to consumer prices was dampened because administered retail fuel prices remained below market levels. Due to its fiscal costs, such a policy is not sustainable, and India, Nepal and Sri Lanka raised retail fuel prices in the second half of the year; other countries in the region are considering similar moves. Due to this increase in retail fuel prices, CPI inflation is expected to rise in early 2005, but then to decline due to continuing monetary tightening. In the countries with rising inflation rates, the cycle of monetary easing has already come to an end, with the first measures to tighten money-supply growth taken towards the end of the year.

Mainly due do strong regional GDP growth, budget deficits declined slightly to around 4-5 per cent of GDP in 2004, following some decline in 2003. Outliers are Nepal, with less than 2 per cent, and India and Sri Lanka, with around 9.5 and 8 per cent, respectively. The low deficit in Nepal is mainly due to the precarious security situation, which constrained development spending in remote areas. In India, the federal structure, which grants states considerable independence, exacerbates the task of deficit reduction, given that around half of the consolidated deficit originates from the states. The single most prominent problem in Sri Lanka remains revenue collection owing to a narrow tax base and widespread tax evasion.

Budget deficits declined in most countries, but remain unsustainably high in India and Sri Lanka...

Figure IV.10.
Inflation in selected South Asian economies, 2003-2004

India (left axis)

Islamic Republic of Iran (right axis)

Nepal (left axis)

Pakistan (left axis)

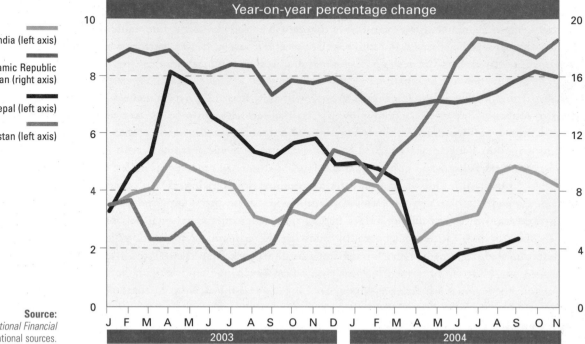

Source:
IMF, *International Financial Statistics;* and national sources.

...while fiscal policies continue to be expansive

National budgets for the fiscal year 2004/2005 provide for a continuation of expansive fiscal policies, with a trend towards improved revenue collection and a stronger focus on development and social spending, especially in the agricultural sector, education and health. Fiscal deficits are likely to overshoot targets, however, and further reforms in the tax system and administration will be needed.

Progress in structural reforms was mixed ...

The record of structural reforms in the region was mixed in 2004. Pakistan successfully completed its programme with the International Monetary Fund (IMF) under the Poverty Reduction and Growth Facility (PRGF), and Nepal also made progress under its PRGF programme. Privatization efforts continued in Pakistan and India in 2004 and are expected to do likewise in 2005, while the new government in Sri Lanka favours restructuring of State-owned enterprises over privatization. Structural reforms in Bangladesh were all but stalled in 2004 owing to a political stalemate which is not expected to be resolved before the next national elections scheduled in 2006.

... and the security situation continues to restrain growth in some countries.

The volatile security situation continues to place a drag on economic growth in Nepal and prospects for renewed peace talks remain unclear. Sri Lankan negotiations were stalled in 2004, although cooperation in relief efforts after the tsunami disaster could provide a window of opportunity. Meanwhile, the peace process between India and Pakistan is on track, allowing for improved economic cooperation, although the status of Kashmir remains unresolved.

East Asia

East Asia has continued to achieve strong economic growth, driven particularly by the positive international economic environment, the expansion of the Chinese economy and increased domestic demand for manufactured goods, especially cars and household electronics. The economic prospects for 2005 are positive, but several factors, such as weaker-than-expected growth in the developed economies or higher commodity prices, may lead to a relative slowdown in the region.

External factors have been important in driving strong growth...

China is expected to remain the engine of growth for East Asia and also to play a major role regarding the global economy. Its GDP is forecast to grow by 8¾ per cent in 2005, down from 9.2 per cent in 2004, as a result of various policy measures aimed at cooling the economy. Policy makers had been relying primarily on such administrative measures as credit restrictions to achieve this goal; continued upward pressure on prices, however, also prompted the use of interest rates as a monetary policy instrument. Both this shift in the general policy approach and upward pressure on prices are expected to lead to further increases in China's interest rates in 2005. However, the effectiveness of interest rates as an instrument to influence economic activity will depend on further measures to introduce more market-based mechanisms in the financial sector, especially with respect to the assessment and control of credit risks by individual banks.

...with decelerating Chinese growth a key factor

Meanwhile, overinvestment in certain sectors, coupled with the low cost of credit, continues to raise concerns about the possibility of achieving a smooth transition to a more sustainable growth path. In addition, China's continued strong economic expansion has further increased its dependency on oil imports and hence its vulnerability to any upward movement in oil prices.

Mirroring the overall trend in economic growth in the region, the expectation of weaker increases in trade, especially at the intraregional level, will result in such economies as Taiwan Province of China, Indonesia and Thailand achieving more moderate, albeit strong, economic growth in 2005, despite the effects of the tsunami catastrophe on the latter two economies. Within the region, the prospects for two economies are especially noteworthy. First, the performance of the economy of Hong Kong Special Administrative Region (SAR) of China will remain especially dependent on developments in China. Private consumption, fixed investment and the positive effects of the implementation of the Individual Visitor Scheme under the Closer Economic Partnership Agreement (CEPA) with China contributed to an acceleration in Hong Kong SAR's economic growth in 2004, but the more subdued growth foreseen for China in 2005 is likely to lead to a slowdown in the expansion of the Hong Kong SAR economy. Second, there was a sharp increase in economic growth in Singapore in 2004 due to a strong expansion of the external sector, robust domestic demand and a one-time recovery from the Severe Acute Respiratory Syndrome (SARS)-induced fall in growth in 2003. However, because of more subdued external demand and the loss of the one-time recovery effect, Singapore's rate of growth is likely to decline in 2005.

Slowdown in trade will adversely affect the region in 2005

With the rise in oil prices resulting in higher import costs, the current-account balances of East Asian economies, while remaining in surplus, narrowed in 2004. They are expected to narrow further in 2005. In addition, several economies in the region have experienced an appreciation in the value of their currencies against the United States dollar. However, since the currencies have largely appreciated in parallel with each other, this has reduced the effect on the relative international competitiveness among the individual economies in the region. As a result, authorities appear to be taking a less forceful stance

Widespread currency appreciation has had little effect on relative competitiveness within the region

regarding interventions in the currency markets. Nevertheless, governments in the region continue to hold large foreign exchange reserves. There is an opportunity cost associated with investing these reserves abroad in the face of the considerable backlog of investment needs in both physical and social infrastructure within the region.

The generally sound economic conditions in the region have had some positive effect on employment. This applies, for example, to Hong Kong SAR, where the end of the deflationary trend was accompanied by a fall in the unemployment rate from its peak in 2003. Overall, however, unemployment remains a problem in several economies, notably in the Philippines and also in Indonesia. In addition, policy makers are faced with the challenge of underemployment which, in turn, is linked to the quality of jobs and employees' expected level of income. In China, for example, the restructuring of state enterprises has increased the pressure on the supply side of the labour market in terms of both unemployment and underemployment.

Inflation has picked up throughout the region because of the strong economic growth and higher commodity prices, but the effect of the increase in oil prices on the general price level has been limited by subsidies. Moreover, stronger currencies in such economies as the Republic of Korea, Singapore and Thailand have helped mitigate the inflationary effect of more expensive dollar-priced imports. Two outliers with regard to inflation are Hong Kong SAR and Viet Nam. The former moved out of deflationary territory in 2004 (although its inflation rate for 2004 as a whole is still likely to be negative), while the latter experienced a strong increase in inflationary pressure because of higher food prices, driven by the renewed outbreak of bird flu disease.

The region is not expected to see a further acceleration in inflation in 2005, although such factors as higher oil prices and increasing concerns about oil price subsidies will put upward pressure on prices. Against this background, policy makers are expected to show a bias towards more restrictive monetary policy measures. In this regard, monetary policy will be characterized by three main issues and challenges.

First, policy makers' possible margin for error is likely to be small. On the one hand, they face the challenge of reducing growth to a more sustainable rate and to limiting inflationary pressure; on the other hand, they seek to limit unemployment, in order to reduce both welfare costs and the potential for increased social tension. The latter objective requires strong economic growth.

Second, policy makers are unlikely to be able to prevent higher oil prices from causing a one-off increase in inflation. However, their main concern is likely to be to prevent higher commodity prices and their initial effects on the general level of prices from feeding through to higher wages, which in turn would increase the probability of a sustained upward trend in prices and inflation.

Third, monetary policy in China continues to suffer from the lack of a conventional monetary policy transmission mechanism, with investment being largely independent of interest rates and determined rather by such factors as the coherence of policy measures taken at the various administrative levels in the country. Against this background, China's policy makers may find it difficult to target and refine their use of such conventional monetary policy instruments as interest rates. This would provide a rationale for authorities to use a combination of both administrative and conventional policy instruments in trying to achieve a more sustainable growth path.

Fiscal policies in the region have taken a less accommodative stance, except in the Republic of Korea, where low domestic demand and high private debt have required a loosening of fiscal measures (such as tax cuts). In 2005, fiscal tightening in the region is expected to continue, although the need to minimize the negative social welfare effects of more contractionary policies will represent a major challenge in several economies, notably in the Philippines and Indonesia. The combination of higher oil prices and oil price subsidies in several economies in the region will place further pressure on governments to consolidate their budgets. Budget consolidation would have direct negative effects on consumers' available income if oil price subsidies were reduced without any compensatory developments (such as an appreciation of the exchange rate).

Overall, this outlook is particularly dependent on the future economic growth path of China. Various policy measures already taken have increased the likelihood that the Chinese economy will achieve a "soft landing", but risks and uncertainties remain and have potential regional and global implications. First, in view of the peg of China's renminbi to the United States dollar and the nature of its financial system, economic policies need to be carefully designed, especially regarding the choice of policy instruments. A continued increase in interest rates, for example, could contribute to a further expansion of China's economy by attracting further investment funds from abroad, leading to upward pressure on the renminbi, interventions by the authorities to ensure the currency peg and hence a further increase in the domestic money supply. Second, policy makers continue to be faced with the question of whether and, if so, how to change China's exchange-rate regime. Any move away from the current peg of the renminbi to the dollar will need to form part of a sequence of wider policy measures, especially with respect to the reform of the banking system and the regulation of capital outflows, in order to avoid macroeconomic instability.

China's economic policies and exchange-rate regime are key to the region's future growth path

Latin America and the Caribbean: Stronger-than-expected recovery

Surpassing earlier forecasts, the Latin American and Caribbean economy expanded by 5.4 per cent in 2004. This brighter outcome is explained primarily by faster growth in Brazil, a strong recovery in Venezuela and continued recovery in Argentina. A number of other countries in the region also performed better than expected. Except for Haiti, the GDP of all countries in the region grew, with the six largest economies growing at over 3 per cent. The prospects for 2005 remain favourable.

Better internal and external conditions supported this broad-based growth. Greater external demand helped exports, especially commodities, but also some manufactures, to continue to increase in 2004. Export growth propelled domestic investment, which was also favoured by lower interest rates, and private consumption began to grow due to some recovery in employment and a slight increase in real wages. The poverty rate fell from 44.3 to an estimated 42.9 per cent.

Both the domestic and external environment favoured growth...

Although the region's economic revival is propelling considerable import growth, there was a trade surplus in 2004, making this the second consecutive year in which the region had a positive current-account balance. For at least the past 50 years, this situation has been unprecedented.

...resulting in an unprecedented consecutive current-account surplus...

These improved external conditions, along with a downward trend in inflation, gave governments room to ease monetary policy, while increased economic activity facilitated fiscal management. Some countries lowered interest rates further during the first half of 2004, in some cases resulting in negative rates in real terms. Inflation remains under control in the region, but the increase in domestic demand and in oil prices, in a context of rising international interest rates, prompted the central banks of a number of countries

...and giving some respite to macroeconomic policies

to raise their policy interest rates later in the year to ensure that their established inflation targets would be met. The increases in Mexico were largest as the inflationary pressures were felt more strongly in that country.

Fiscal policy in the region continues to be geared to increasing central governments' primary surpluses. Boosted by the upturn in tax receipts due to the faster pace of economic activity, the region's primary surplus averaged about 0.6 per cent of GDP (2.0 per cent as a weighted average). In general, governments thus took the opportunity to reduce public debt and to thereby increase their options for future countercyclical policies. As a regional simple average, public debt fell from 64 to 59 per cent of GDP for the public sector. However, debt levels remain very high (above 60 per cent of GDP) in a number of countries.

During 2004, the region's currencies appreciated against the dollar, but real effective exchange rates had a mixed trajectory: appreciation in Brazil, Chile and Colombia, but depreciation in Argentina and Mexico. In most cases, real effective exchange rates remained relatively stable throughout the year at levels similar to the average in 2003. Moreover, in 2004 there was less disparity in the behaviour of exchange rates across countries, as measured by changes in the standard deviation of the monthly average.

Domestic demand should lead growth in 2005

The region will continue to grow in 2005 but will probably face a less favourable international environment that is expected to cause its GDP growth to decelerate to 4 per cent. Assuming that the international scene will be characterized by a smooth slowing of the major economies and that the signs of the recovery of domestic demand prove to be sustainable, the region, and particularly its bigger countries, could find themselves in a new situation where a smaller contribution of external demand to growth might be offset by stronger domestic demand.

Among the conditions that would sustain growth in 2005 are good macroeconomic conditions, comprising relatively low real interest rates, solid fiscal stances, low inflation rates, competitive exchange rates and another current-account surplus. Under these circumstances, macroeconomic policies should still enjoy some degree of freedom for manoeuvre. In addition, domestic demand accounts for over 80 per cent of total demand, (expressed in 1995 dollars) so that only a small upward shift in domestic demand would be required to compensate for a slight weakening of external demand.

Prior to 2004, the growth of employment and wages had been limited, repressing consumption. In 2004, the regional unemployment rate fell from 10.7 to 10.0 per cent and the relatively high job creation stimulated consumer expenditure (see box IV.1). Continued overall growth in 2005 is expected to revive wages, which also would boost consumption. Increasing consumption would spur investment, creating a virtuous circle of growth in some of the larger countries of the region. In addition, in this scenario, external demand would continue to contribute to the region's growth, but with diminished strength. In this case, the dynamics of internal demand should be strong enough to sustain regional growth so that, although reduced, it will remain high.

Some risks may dampen growth, but...

However, downside risks do exist. External factors, such as unexpectedly sharp increases in the price of oil, might accelerate inflation and oblige the monetary authorities to dampen domestic demand through increases in interest rates. If the United States external deficit leads to larger increases in its interest rates, this would not only put pressure on monetary policy in the region but might also affect external financing for some heavily indebted countries. Slower-than-expected growth of the United States and/or China might weaken external demand even further. On the domestic front, if the recovery of domestic

Box IV.1

Recent trends in Latin American labour markets

Although it decreased in 2004, the unemployment rate in Latin America increased from 7.2 per cent in 1991 to a maximum of 10.6 per cent in 2002 despite the improvement in the region's economic growth compared to the 1980s.[a] There are a number of reasons for this poor performance.

Two basic facts are central to the region's labour market performance over this period. First, the average rate of economic growth for the region between 1990 and 2004 was 2.6 per cent which is modest, but better than the performance of the "lost decade" of the 1980s. Second, labour supply has expanded strongly for two reasons: the working age population grew by 2.3 per cent annually during this period and there was increasing participation of women in the labour force as a result of longer-term economic, social and cultural transformations.

Employment in Latin America has been strongly positively correlated with economic growth, falling in years of low growth and increasing in a recovery. However, the economic reforms of the 1980s and 1990s reduced the labour intensity of growth. These reforms did not produce the expected results for several reasons: slower-than-expected growth of output, the labour-intensive sectors were among the least dynamic, labour participation rates increased, and the assumption that the region had a comparative advantage in unskilled labour was at least partially untrue.[b] Another factor was the exchange-rates appreciation that characterized many countries during the 1980s.

Although wage jobs are strongly correlated to economic growth, non-wage employment in the informal sector has lost its countercyclical capacity to absorb the unemployed from the formal sector in slow times. This reflects two trends in the informal job sector. First, some self-employment is generated when there are perceived to be income opportunities during an economic recovery and, second, in certain countries, the informal sector's ability to absorb part of the labour force is weakened after long periods of sluggish economic growth and expanding informality. This relative "saturation" of the informal sector, with its corresponding impact on the average income in this sector, reduces the opportunity cost of being unemployed, especially for a labour force with a rising level of education, as is the case in Latin America.

Furthermore, the pro-cyclical nature of the participation rate smooths changes in the unemployment rate. When unemployment rises, some workers leave the labour market and become inactive, whereas the labour force increases in times of growth, limiting the positive effect of job creation on the unemployment rate. During most of the 1990s and the present decade, this pro-cyclical trend has taken the form of periods of interruption in the growing participation of women and a reduction of male participation as younger people decide to remain in the educational system in times of low expectations.

Strong wage growth, on the other hand, has not hindered job creation as a whole, even if in certain situations, especially in a context of declining inflation, nominal wage inflexibility and minimum wage policies may have had an adverse effect on job creation for specific groups. In general, the evolution of real wages in the formal sector has reflected the sector's productivity growth, with variations influenced by crisis, inflation and economic recovery. For 13 countries, the median annual increase in real wages between 1990 and 2003 was 1.9 per cent. At the same time, the minimum wage policy has been conservative in most countries, with an annual real growth of 0.2 per cent (median of 19 countries).

The present high level of Latin American unemployment therefore appears to be the result of sluggish economic growth, the loss of labour-intensive growth and the weakening of the informal sector's countercyclical function as a "buffer" in times of low labour demand. Macroeconomic policies to foster labour-intensive economic growth, adjustments in the regulation of the labour markets and a modernization of labour market policies, with an emphasis on underprivileged groups, should help improve the performance of the region's labour markets.

a   In recent years, changes in the methods of measurement have led to higher reported unemployment rates in several countries. The cited numbers already take into account adjustments in Brazil, while new information on Argentina and the announced adjustments in Mexico will further increase the regional unemployment rate.

b   Barbara Stallings and Jurgen Weller "Job Creation in Latin America in the 1990s: The Foundation for Social Policy", ECLAC, Santiago, July, 2001.

demand proves to be temporary, the slowdown of the global economy would cause the region's economic growth to lose momentum quickly.

... the trade balance
will remain positive,
although smaller

Despite these different scenarios, it is expected that the surplus on the region's trade balance will shrink and, consequently, that the surplus on the balance-of-payments current account will also decline, owing not only to the smaller trade surplus but also to the higher payments for financial services. At the same time, region-wide inflation, after a transitional increase in early 2004, will probably continue its slow decrease, to around 6 per cent in 2005 from 6.5 per cent in 2004. With respect to the exchange rate, policy makers are unlikely to change their stance of maintaining real parities at levels similar to those prevailing in 2004.

The countries of the region continue to demonstrate a widespread commitment to maintaining cautious fiscal policies, although significant differences are likely to be observed between oil-exporting and oil-importing countries, given the large oil revenues and expansive policies adopted by the former. The present favourable conditions offer an opportunity for governments to take countercyclical and other measures to become less vulnerable and to achieve a more sustainable growth path.

Notes

1   Joaquín Almunia, European Union Commissioner for Economic and Monetary Affairs, "Strengthening Economic Governance and Improving the Stability and Growth Pact", Brussels, 3 September 2004 (available from http://europa.eu.int/rapid/pressReleasesAction.do?reference=SPEECH/04/387/ &format=HTML&aged=0&language=EN&guiLanguage=en).

2   Excluding humanitarian needs and industrial rehabilitation, the cost of repairing Iraq's oil facilities and power plants has been estimated at about $25 billion. Iraq's total external debt has been estimated at $383 billion, of which $199 billion is outstanding liabilities (such as war reparations from the first Gulf war, $45 billion of which have been confirmed by the United Nations Compensation Commission); $127 billion is foreign bilateral debt (including $47 billion of accrued interest); and $57 billion is owed on contracts for emergency and communications deals. On 23 November 2004, creditor countries agreed to cancel 80 per cent of Iraq's bilateral debt (see chapter III).

Annex:
Statistical
Tables

List of tables

Table A.1.

Developed market economies: rates of growth of real GDP, rates of inflation and unemployment, 2003-2005

	Annual percentage change								
	Growth[a]			Inflation[b]			Unemployment[c,d,e]		
	2003	2004[f]	2005[g]	2003	2004[f]	2005[g]	2003	2004[f]	2005[g]
Developed economies	2.2	3.4	2½	1.7	1.9	1½	..	..	..
United States	3.1	4.2	3	2.3	2.6	1¾	6.0	5.5	5¼
Canada	1.7	2.7	2¾	2.8	1.6	2	7.6	7.2	7
Japan	2.5	3.6	1¾	-0.3	-0.2	¼	5.3	4.7	4¾
Australia	2.6	3.4	2¾	2.8	2.7	2½	6.1	5.7	6
New Zealand	3.4	4.0	2½	1.8	2.4	2	4.6	4.6	4¾
European Union	1.2	2.3	2¼	2.1	2.2	2	..	..	..
EU-15	1.1	2.2	2	2.1	2.2	2	8.1	8.1	8
Euro Zone	0.6	2.0	2	2.0	2.0	1¾	8.9	8.9	8¾
Austria	0.7	2.1	2½	1.3	2.0	2	4.3	4.5	4¼
Belgium	1.1	2.5	2½	1.5	1.9	1½	7.9	7.5	7¼
Finland	2.0	3.0	2¼	0.9	0.1	1½	9.0	9.1	8¾
France	0.5	2.3	2	2.1	1.9	1½	9.4	9.6	9½
Germany	-0.1	1.8	1½	1.0	1.6	1¼	9.6	9.9	9¾
Greece	4.5	3.9	3¼	3.5	3.1	3	9.3	8.8	8½
Ireland	3.7	5.1	5¾	3.5	1.6	2	4.6	4.9	5
Italy	0.4	1.1	1¾	2.7	2.5	2½	8.6	8.1	7¾
Luxembourg	2.1	2.0	3	2.0	2.2	2	3.7	4.1	4¼
Netherlands	-0.9	1.2	1¼	2.1	1.3	1¼	3.8	5.2	5¾
Portugal	-1.2	0.9	2	3.3	2.7	2¼	6.2	6.3	6
Spain	2.4	2.4	2½	3.0	2.9	2½	11.3	10.9	10¾
Other	2.7	2.9	2½	2.7	2.8	2½	5.1	4.8	4½
Denmark	0.5	2.6	2½	2.1	1.5	2¼	5.6	5.9	5¾
Sweden	2.3	1.0	1¾	1.9	0.9	1	5.6	6.3	5½
United Kingdom	3.0	3.3	2¾	2.9	3.2	2¾	5.0	4.5	4¼
EU-10	3.7	4.9	4½	1.9	4.1	3¼	..	..	..
EU-8	3.9	4.9	4½	1.9	4.2	3¼	..	..	..
Czech Republic	3.7	3.8	4	0.1	3.0	2½	9.3	10.5	9¾
Estonia	5.1	6.2	5¾	1.3	4.5	3	6.1	5.5	5
Hungary	2.9	3.6	3¾	4.7	7.0	4½	8.4	8.2	8
Latvia	7.5	7.5	6¾	2.9	7.0	5	8.0	7.8	7
Lithuania	9.7	6.8	6½	-1.2	1.4	2	9.2	8.8	8
Poland	3.8	5.6	4½	0.7	3.5	3	20.0	19.5	19
Slovakia	4.5	5.0	5¼	8.6	7.5	5½	15.2	14.6	14¾
Slovenia	2.5	3.8	4	5.6	3.5	3	11.2	10.5	10¼

Table A.1 (continued)

	Growth[a]			Inflation[b]			Unemployment[c,d,e]		
	2003	2004[f]	2005[g]	2003	2004[f]	2005[g]	2003	2004[f]	2005[g]
Other	0.9	2.4	4	3.2	2.5	2½	..	..	..
Cyprus	2.0	3.2	3½	4.1	2.1	2½	..	..	..
Malta	-1.7	0.5	4¾	1.3	3.2	2¼	7.6	7.3	6¾
Other Europe	0.0	2.3	2½	1.6	0.6	1¼	4.2	4.5	4½
Iceland	4.0	4.4	4½	2.1	2.3	2¾	4.1	4.1	3½
Norway	0.4	3.3	3¼	2.5	0.4	1	4.5	4.4	4
Switzerland	-0.5	1.5	2	0.9	0.7	1¼	4.1	4.6	4¾

Source: UN/DESA, based on IMF, *International Financial Statistics* and OECD.

a   Data for country groups are weighted averages, where weights are based on GDP in 2000 prices and exchange rates.

b   Data for country groups are weighted averages, where weights for each year are 2000 GDP in U.S. dollars.

c   Unemployment data are standardized by OECD for comparability among countries and over time, in conformity with the definitions of the International Labour Office (see OECD, Standardized Unemployment Rates: Sources and Methods (Paris, 1985)).

d   Data for country groups are weighted averages, where labour force is used for weights.

e   Greece and Malta are not standardized.

f   Partly estimated.

g   Forecast.

Table A.2.
Major developed economies: quarterly indicators, 2002-2004

	2002 quarters				2003 quarters				2004 quarters		
	I	II	III	IV	I	II	III	IV	I	II	III
Growth of gross domestic product[a] (percentage change in seasonally adjusted data from preceding quarter)											
Canada	5.8	3.8	2.7	1.6	2.8	-0.7	1.4	3.3	2.7	3.9	3.2
France	3.2	2.0	1.0	-0.8	0.7	-1.9	4.1	2.4	2.6	2.5	0.3
Germany	0.1	0.8	1.1	-0.1	-1.4	-0.8	1.1	1.2	1.7	1.7	0.4
Italy	0.8	0.9	1.1	1.7	-0.4	-0.4	1.6	0.0	2.0	1.6	1.6
Japan	-2.9	5.8	2.9	0.7	0.4	4.3	3.1	6.0	7.6	-0.4	0.6
United Kingdom	1.2	1.6	3.6	1.6	0.8	2.8	3.5	4.3	3.1	3.8	1.6
United States	4.7	1.9	3.4	1.3	2.0	3.1	8.2	4.1	4.5	3.3	4.0
Memo items:											
Major developed economies	2.1	2.7	2.8	1.0	1.1	2.4	5.3	3.9	4.6	2.3	2.4
Euro zone	1.6	1.6	1.2	0.0	0.0	-0.8	2.0	1.6	2.8	2.0	1.2
Unemployment rate[b] (percentage of total labour force)											
Canada	7.8	7.6	7.6	7.6	7.5	7.7	7.9	7.5	7.4	7.2	7.1
France	8.6	8.9	9.1	9.1	9.2	9.4	9.5	9.6	9.6	9.5	9.6
Germany	8.3	8.5	8.8	9.1	9.5	9.7	9.7	9.6	9.6	9.8	8.9
Italy	9.0	9.0	9.0	8.9	8.8	8.7	8.6	8.5	8.5	..	..
Japan	5.3	5.4	5.4	5.4	5.4	5.4	5.2	5.1	4.9	4.6	4.8
United Kingdom	5.1	5.1	5.2	5.0	5.1	5.0	4.9	4.8	4.7	4.7	4.6
United States	5.7	5.8	5.7	5.9	5.8	6.1	6.1	5.9	5.6	5.6	5.5
Memo items:											
Major developed economies	6.4	6.5	6.6	6.6	6.7	6.8	6.8	6.6	6.5	5.8	5.7
Euro zone	8.1	8.2	8.5	8.6	8.7	8.8	8.9	8.9	8.9	8.9	8.9
Growth of consumer prices[c] (percentage change from preceding quarter)											
Canada	2.7	6.1	4.3	2.1	5.4	-0.5	1.5	0.5	2.0	4.7	0.8
France	2.7	3.5	0.8	1.9	3.6	1.4	1.0	2.7	2.1	3.7	0.6
Germany	3.8	0.8	0.6	-0.4	3.7	-0.4	1.2	0.3	3.1	2.7	1.5
Italy	3.5	3.0	1.9	2.7	3.3	2.9	2.1	1.9	2.3	3.1	1.7
Japan	-2.8	1.8	-0.7	-0.4	1.6	1.8	-0.7	-0.7	-0.9	1.1	0.1
United Kingdom	0.2	5.1	1.4	3.6	2.3	4.8	1.0	2.5	2.0	5.6	2.4
United States	1.4	4.4	1.7	1.3	4.1	1.5	2.0	0.1	3.7	5.8	1.4
Memo items:											
Major developed economies	0.8	3.5	1.1	1.0	2.6	1.6	1.2	0.4	2.2	4.2	1.1
Euro zone	1.5	4.1	0.4	2.2	2.5	2.8	0.4	2.3	1.4	4.1	0.7

Sources: UN/DESA, based on data of IMF, *International Finacial Statistics;* Organisation for Economic Cooperation and Development (OECD) and national authorities.

a   Expressed at annual rate (total is weighted average with weights being annual GDP valued at 2000 prices and exchange rates).
b   Seasonally adjusted data as standardized by OECD.
c   Expressed at annual rate.

Table A.3.
Economies in transition: rates of growth of real GDP, rates of inflation and unemployment, 2003-2005

	Annual percentage change								
	Growth[a]			Inflation[b]			Unemployment		
	2003	2004[c]	2005[d]	2003	2004[c]	2005[d]	2003	2004[c]	2005[d]
Economies in transition	7.0	7.1	6	12.2	10.3	9	..	..	..
Southern and Eastern Europe	4.2	5.8	4¾	8.4	7.6	6¼	..	..	..
Albania	6.0	6.0	6½	2.4	3.0	2½	14.0	15.0	15
Bosnia and Herzegovina	3.2	4.0	4½	0.1	0.0	½	42.0	42.0	40
Bulgaria	4.3	5.0	4½	2.3	6.5	4	14.3	12.5	11¾
Croatia	4.3	3.8	4	2.2	2.0	2½	19.5	18.5	17½
Romania	4.9	7.5	5	15.3	12.0	9	7.2	6.5	6½
Serbia and Montenegro	1.5	6.0	5	9.6	9.0	10½	28.0	32.0	30
The former Yugoslav Republic of Macedonia	3.4	2.0	3	1.2	0.0	1	43.0	45.0	43
Commonwealth of Independent States	7.6	7.3	6	13.0	10.9	9½	..	..	..
Armenia	13.9	10.0	7	4.7	6.3	4½	9.8	9.6	9
Azerbaijan	11.2	9.5	11	2.1	6.0	4	1.4	1.4	1¼
Belarus	6.8	10.0	9	28.5	18.0	14	3.1	2.8	2½
Georgia	11.1	6.0	5	4.9	5.5	5½	11.5	11.5	11½
Kazakhstan	9.3	9.3	8	6.6	7.5	8	1.8	1.8	1¾
Kyrgyzstan	6.7	6.5	7	3.1	4.5	4½	3.0	3.0	2¾
Republic of Moldova	6.3	8.0	5½	11.7	12.0	9½	1.2	1.8	1½
Russian Federation	7.3	6.6	5¾	13.6	11.0	9½	8.1	8.0	7¾
Tajikistan	10.2	11.0	8¼	16.3	8.0	7	2.4	2.2	2¼
Turkmenistan	6.8	6.0	7	15.3	10.0	12	..	..	..
Ukraine	9.4	11.5	6½	5.2	9.5	8½	3.2	3.6	3½
Uzbekistan	4.4	7.6	6½	24.0	15.0	15	0.3	0.4	½

Sources: UN/DESA and Economic Commision for Europe (ECE).

a   Data for country groups are weighted averages, where weights are based on GDP in 2000 prices and exchange rates.
b   Data for country groups are weighted averages, where weights for each year are 2000 GDP in U.S. dollars.
c   Partly estimated.
d   Forecast.

Table A.4.
Major economies in transition: quarterly indicators, 2002-2004

	Annual percentage change[a]										
	2002 quarters				2003 quarters				2004 quarters		
	I	II	III	IV	I	II	III	IV	I	II	III
	Rates of growth of gross domestic product										
Belarus	4.1	5.8	4.7	5.5	5.6	4.7	7.3	8.9	9.3	11.0	11.7
Kazakhstan	10.6	7.5	9.4	11.4	10.5	9.6	7.7	9.2	9.0	9.2	9.1
Romania	3.5	5.6	4.6	5.6	4.4	4.3	5.4	4.6	6.1	7.0	10.2
Russian Federation	3.8	4.3	4.4	6.0	7.5	7.9	6.5	7.6	7.5	7.4	6.4
Ukraine	5.8	5.0	5.6	4.8	8.4	10.0	6.8	12.1	12.3	13.2	14.3
	Change in consumer prices										
Belarus	47.2	44.6	43.1	37.4	30.8	28.3	28.3	27.0	22.4	19.7	17.0
Kazakhstan	5.7	5.5	6.4	6.4	7.2	6.5	5.8	7.1	6.7	6.9	7.6
Romania	26.8	24.2	21.3	18.5	16.7	14.9	15.1	14.9	13.6	12.3	11.8
Russian Federation	18.0	15.8	15.1	15.1	14.6	14.0	13.5	12.5	10.8	10.3	11.1
Ukraine	3.7	0.8	-0.9	-0.5	2.2	4.5	6.5	7.8	7.4	7.4	9.6

Sources: UN/DESA, based on data of Economic Commission for Europe (ECE).

a   Percentage change from the corresponding period of the preceding year.

Table A.5.

Developing countries: rates of growth of real GDP and rates of inflation, 2003-2005

	Annual percentage change					
	Growth[a]			Inflation[b]		
	2003	2004[c]	2005[d]	2003	2004[c]	2005[d]
Developing countries[e] *of which:*	4.6	6.2	5½	6.3	5.6	5½
Latin America and the Caribbean	1.7	5.4	4	10.5	6.5	6
Net fuel exporters	0.6	5.3	3¾			
Net fuel importers	2.6	5.5	4¼			
Africa	4.0	4.5	4¾	11.2	11.8	10¼
Net fuel exporters	5.3	4.6	5			
Net fuel importers	2.9	4.4	4½			
Western Asia	5.0	5.5	4½	8.9	4.4	5¾
Net fuel exporters	5.9	4.3	4			
Net fuel importers	4.0	6.7	5			
East and South Asia *of which:*	6.2	7.0	6½	2.8	4.3	4¼
East Asia	6.0	7.2	6¾	1.9	3.7	3½
South Asia	6.7	6.3	6¼	5.7	6.4	6½
Memo items:						
Least developed countries	4.1	5.2	5½	13.7	11.4	13
East Asia (excluding China)	3.7	5.6	5	2.5	3.4	3½
Major developing economies						
Argentina	8.7	8.2	5	13.4	4.4	7
Brazil	0.6	5.2	4	14.7	6.5	6
Chile	3.3	5.8	6	2.8	1.1	3
China	9.1	9.2	8¾	1.2	4.0	3½
Colombia	4.1	3.7	3	7.1	6.0	5
Egypt	2.9	3.2	3¾	4.5	5.3	3½
Hong Kong SAR[f]	3.2	7.0	6	-2.6	1.0	1½
India	7.0	6.4	6½	3.8	4.7	5
Indonesia	4.4	4.5	4½	5.1	6.0	5½
Iran (Islamic Republic of)	6.7	6.6	6¼	16.5	15.6	15
Israel	1.3	3.6	3¾	0.7	0.2	2½
Korea, Republic of	3.0	4.9	4½	3.6	3.7	3½
Malaysia	5.3	7.0	6	1.1	2.0	2½
Mexico	1.2	4.1	3½	4.5	4.7	4½
Nigeria	10.2	4.0	3	14.0	16.5	13
Pakistan	5.6	6.2	5¾	2.9	4.6	4½

Table A.5 (continued)						
	Growth[a]			Inflation[b]		
	2003	2004[c]	2005[d]	2003	2004[c]	2005[d]
Peru	3.8	4.6	4	2.3	3.7	2½
Philippines	4.7	4.9	5¼	3.0	5.2	5
Saudi Arabia	7.2	3.3	2½	0.6	0.8	¼
Singapore	1.1	8.1	5½	0.5	1.7	1½
South Africa	1.9	3.0	3	5.9	4.9	3
Taiwan Province of China	3.2	5.9	4¼	-0.3	1.6	1½
Thailand	6.8	6.0	5½	1.8	2.0	2½
Turkey	5.8	9.0	6	25.3	10.8	14¼
Venezuela	-9.7	18.0	5	31.1	21.6	20

Source: UN/DESA, based on IMF, International Financial Statistics.

a   Data for country groups are weighted averages, where weights are based on GDP in 2000 prices and exchange rates.

b   Data for country groups are weighted averages, where weights for each year are 2000 GDP in U.S. dollars.

c   Partly estimated.

d   Forecast.

e   Covering countries that account for 98 per cent of the population of all developing countries.

f   Special Administrative Region of China.

Table A.6.
Major developing countries: quarterly indicators of growth, unemployment and inflation, 2002-2004

	Annual percentage change										
	2002 quarters				2003 quarters				2004 quarters		
	I	II	III	IV	I	II	III	IV	I	II	III
	Rates of growth of gross domestic product[a]										
Argentina	-16.3	-13.5	-9.8	-3.4	5.4	7.7	10.2	11.7	11.3	7.0	8.0
Brazil	-0.6	1.0	2.4	3.7	1.8	-0.1	-0.4	0.7	3.9	5.5	6.2
Chile	1.1	2.2	2.7	3.5	3.7	3.0	3.1	3.3	4.6	5.3	6.8
China	7.6	8.0	8.1	8.1	9.9	6.7	9.6	9.9	9.7	9.7	9.5
Colombia	0.1	2.3	2.2	2.5	4.2	2.5	4.2	5.2	4.0	4.5	2.6
Ecuador	1.3	3.9	5.0	3.5	3.4	-0.8	2.1	6.0	6.4	10.0	7.0
Hong Kong SAR[b]	-1.0	0.4	3.0	4.8	4.4	-0.6	4.0	4.9	7.0	12.1	7.8
India	6.3	5.1	5.5	2.0	4.1	5.3	8.6	10.5	8.2	7.4	6.6
Indonesia	2.4	4.1	4.6	3.6	4.5	3.6	4.0	4.4	4.5	4.3	5.0
Israel	-4.1	-3.3	-0.4	0.7	1.2	1.4	1.2	1.6	1.9	3.2	3.5
Korea, Republic of	6.5	7.0	6.8	7.5	3.7	2.2	2.4	3.9	5.3	5.5	4.6
Malaysia	1.0	4.1	5.8	5.6	4.6	4.6	5.3	6.6	7.8	8.2	6.8
Mexico	-2.2	2.0	1.8	1.9	2.3	0.2	0.4	2.0	3.7	3.9	4.4
Philippines	3.8	4.1	3.8	5.8	4.5	4.0	5.1	4.5	6.5	6.2	6.3
Singapore	-1.5	3.8	3.8	3.0	1.6	-3.9	1.8	4.9	7.5	12.5	7.5
South Africa	3.0	3.8	2.9	2.4	1.5	1.1	1.6	1.5	1.9	2.5	3.8
Taiwan Province of China	0.9	3.7	5.2	4.5	3.5	-0.2	4.0	5.7	6.7	7.7	5.3
Thailand	3.9	5.1	6.2	6.3	7.3	6.5	6.6	7.8	6.6	6.3	7.0
Turkey	2.1	8.9	7.9	11.4	8.1	3.9	4.8	5.4	10.1	13.4	4.5
Venezuela	-3.8	-9.1	-5.6	-16.7	-25.0	-5.2	-6.7	7.0	32.8	15.1	15.8
	Unemployment rate[c]										
Argentina[d]	..	21.5	..	17.8	20.4	17.8	16.3	14.5	14.4	14.8	13.2
Brazil	12.2	12.0	11.7	10.9	11.6	12.7	12.9	12.0	12.2	12.3	11.2
Chile	8.8	9.5	9.7	9.6	8.2	9.1	9.4	7.4	8.1	9.6	9.7
Colombia	16.4	15.8	15.3	15.1	15.2	14.0	14.3	13.1	15.3	14.1	12.8
Hong Kong SAR[b]	7.2	7.7	7.2	7.3	7.9	8.6	7.9	7.3	7.2	7.0	6.8
Indonesia	8.1	..	9.1	..	..	..	..	..	..	..	..
Israel	10.4	10.3	10.4	10.2	10.6	10.5	11.0	10.9	10.7	10.5	10.2
Korea, Republic of	3.7	3.0	2.8	2.9	3.6	3.3	3.3	3.4	3.8	3.3	3.6
Malaysia	3.7	3.8	3.2	3.2	3.8	4.0	3.4	3.2	3.8	3.7	3.4
Mexico	2.8	2.6	2.9	2.5	2.8	3.0	3.8	3.5	3.9	3.6	4.0
Philippines	10.3	13.9	11.2	10.2	10.6	12.2	12.6	10.1	11.0	11.4	11.4
Singapore	3.7	5.2	3.8	4.7	3.7	5.4	4.9	4.9	4.5	4.5	4.5
Taiwan Province of China	5.1	5.0	5.3	5.2	5.1	5.0	5.1	4.8	4.5	4.4	4.6
Thailand	3.2	2.9	1.8	1.8	2.8	2.5	1.5	1.8	2.8	2.4	2.2
Turkey	11.8	9.3	9.6	11.0	12.3	10.0	9.4	10.3	12.4	9.3	9.5
Uruguay	14.7	15.4	17.6	19.2	18.6	17.5	16.0	15.4	13.9	13.1	13.3
Venezuela	15.5	15.8	16.5	16.2	19.7	18.9	17.9	15.6	17.3	16.1	15.0

	2002 quarters				2003 quarters				2004 quarters		
	I	II	III	IV	I	II	III	IV	I	II	III
	Growth of consumer prices[a]										
Argentina	4.2	23.3	36.0	40.3	35.7	14.5	5.2	3.7	2.4	4.1	5.4
Brazil	7.6	7.8	7.6	10.6	15.6	16.9	15.2	11.4	6.8	5.5	6.9
Chile	2.4	2.2	2.4	2.9	3.8	3.7	2.7	1.1	0.0	0.4	1.5
China	-2.8	-3.2	-2.7	-1.8	-1.6	-1.2	-2.0	-1.4	-0.6	0.1	2.0
Colombia	6.6	5.9	6.0	6.8	7.4	7.6	7.1	6.4	6.2	5.6	6.0
Ecuador	14.7	13.2	12.4	9.9	9.7	8.2	7.5	6.5	3.9	3.2	2.0
Hong Kong SAR[b]	-2.6	-3.1	-3.4	-3.0	-2.0	-2.5	-3.6	-2.3	-1.8	-0.9	0.8
India	5.1	4.5	4.0	4.0	3.8	4.7	3.4	3.4	4.0	2.7	4.2
Indonesia	14.1	11.5	10.5	10.0	10.5	9.7	8.8	7.2	4.9	6.7	7.0
Israel	3.8	5.7	6.5	6.7	5.2	1.4	-1.6	-2.1	-2.5	-0.7	0.0
Korea, Republic of	2.5	2.7	2.6	3.3	4.1	3.3	3.1	3.6	3.2	3.4	4.3
Malaysia	1.4	1.9	2.1	1.8	1.3	0.9	1.0	1.0	0.9	1.2	1.5
Mexico	4.7	4.8	5.2	5.3	5.4	4.7	4.1	4.0	4.3	4.3	4.8
Philippines	3.5	3.2	2.6	2.4	2.9	3.0	3.1	3.1	3.5	4.6	6.4
Singapore	-0.8	-0.4	-0.4	0.1	0.7	0.2	0.5	0.7	1.4	1.8	1.7
South Africa	-36.4	-30.5	-12.1	2.5	14.8	-0.8	-22.4	-25.7	-20.6	-9.5	0.0
Taiwan Province of China	-0.1	0.0	-0.2	-0.5	-0.2	-0.1	-0.6	-0.2	0.5	1.2	3.2
Thailand	0.6	0.2	0.3	1.4	2.0	1.8	1.9	1.6	1.9	2.6	3.3
Turkey	70.3	47.0	39.5	31.6	27.6	30.0	25.1	19.4	14.1	9.3	0.0
Venezuela	14.6	18.9	24.8	30.6	35.5	34.2	29.5	26.3	24.0	22.4	21.5

Sources: IMF, *International Financial Statistics,* and national authorities.

a   Percentage change from the corresponding quarter of the previous year.
b   Special Administrative Region of China.
c   Reflects national definitions and coverage. Not comparable across economies.
d   Data is reported in May and October in 2002.

Table A.7.

World trade: rates of growth of volumes and values, 2003-2005

	Exports			Imports		
	2003	2004	2005	2003	2004	2005
Volume						
World	6.8	10.9	8½	5.6	10.2	7¾
of which:						
North America	1.1	8.7	9	4.5	9.8	5¼
European Union[a]	1.5	6.9	6½	4.3	7.6	7
Japan	9.4	13.5	5¾	5.0	6.7	2
Commonwealth of Independent States	11.4	10.0	7	15.8	14.2	14½
Latin America and the Caribbean	6.3	10.6	5	1.6	14.1	8
Africa	11.8	8.0	7¼	7.2	8.0	8½
Western Asia	8.5	6.7	6	4.7	7.8	12
East Asia	20.1	19.3	13	11.0	17.8	13
South Asia	10.0	12.7	11½	10.0	15.1	14¾
Memo items:						
Central and Eastern Europe and Baltic States	9.7	14.5	11½	9.6	15.0	11¼
Western Europe	1.0	6.2	6	3.8	6.8	6½
China	34.4	29.0	18	31.1	32.0	21¾
Value						
World	16.3	18.5	10¼	15.4	19.0	9¼
of which:						
North America	5.6	12.9	9¼	7.3	13.2	6½
European Union[a]	18.7	18.2	9	20.3	20.2	8½
Japan	8.0	12.3	3¾	4.6	11.3	2½
Commonwealth of Independent States	24.9	29.0	28	21.4	31.0	25½
Latin America and the Caribbean	8.9	21.5	7¼	5.7	18.0	10½
Africa	25.2	23.5	7¼	18.9	16.9	8¼
Western Asia	16.0	21.2	5	14.5	18.7	8
East Asia	23.1	22.6	14½	18.0	24.5	14¼
South Asia	13.0	23.3	17	15.9	19.3	19¾
Memo items:						
Central and Eastern Europe and Baltic States	29.0	31.0	19	27.4	28.0	18
Western Europe	17.8	17.3	8	19.5	19.2	7½
China	34.6	32.0	19½	39.9	38.0	22½

Source:
Project LINK.

a   All figures for the European Union take into account the 10 new member states that joined in 2004.

Table A.8.
Commodity price index, 2001-2004 (December)

Index 2000 = 100				
	2001	2002	2003	2004[a]
Combined index, non-fuel				
Dollar	89.6	100.0	111.3	122.6
SDR	92.8	96.4	98.8	104.8
Food and tropical beverages	91.4	100.0	99.0	106.7
Tropical beverages	87.8	112.2	108.2	126.5
Cocoa	166.4	251.7	202.5	206.9
Coffee	90.0	107.0	109.0	140.0
Tea	66.7	74.9	83.5	78.6
Food	91.6	97.7	96.9	103.1
Bananas	117.5	127.5	84.2	112.7
Maize	103.1	109.7	120.7	90.5
Rice	97.3	100.5	107.1	142.4
Sugar	78.1	79.3	62.7	81.4
Wheat	95.4	126.0	129.8	123.7
Vegetable oilseeds and oils	114.1	150.0	176.6	159.4
Palm oil	127.5	175.5	192.5	163.4
Soybeans	87.1	111.1	153.0	119.8
Groundnut oil	95.8	121.2	164.7	162.6
Agricultural raw materials	84.4	99.1	124.8	125.7
Cotton	65.1	83.8	111.7	72.4
Rubber	78.9	137.0	203.5	203.9
Minerals, ores and metals	85.8	90.8	116.7	145.0
Aluminium	85.9	87.8	99.3	115.9
Copper	79.5	86.2	119.0	168.7
Iron ore	104.5	103.4	112.2	131.7
Lead	104.6	96.0	149.5	209.2
Nickel	72.0	98.3	193.6	192.0
Tin	76.8	80.9	115.7	173.2
Zinc	71.3	75.5	91.1	104.2
Memo items:				
Manufactured export prices of developed economies	98.0	99.0	107.0	..
Real prices, non-fuel commodities	99.1	96.3	96.2	..
OPEC basket	83.8	88.3	101.8	..

Sources:
UN/DESA and UNCTAD, Monthly Commodity Price Bulletin; Middle East Economic Survey (http://www.mees.com/Energy_Tables/basket.htm).

a　Calculations for 2004 are based on October 2004 over December 2003 data.

Table A.9.
Distribution of stock of foreign direct investment in services by country groups, 1990 and 2002

	Percentage				
	1990		2002		
Sector/industry	Developed countries	Developing countries	Developed countries	Developing countries	Central and Eastern Europe
Inward FDI stock					
Total services	83	17	72	25	3
Electricity, gas and water	70	30	63	32	6
Construction	77	23	47	45	8
Trade	90	10	78	19	4
Hotels and restaurants	87	13	70	26	3
Transport, storage and communications	58	43	71	22	7
Finance	76	24	77	20	3
Business activities	93	7	61	38	1
Public administration and defence	..	..	99	1	-
Education	100	..	92	4	4
Health and social services	100	..	67	32	1
Community, social and personal service activities	100	..	91	8	2
Other services	85	15	61	36	3
Outward FDI stock					
Total services	99	1	90	10	-
Electricity, gas and water	100	..	100	0	-
Construction	99	1	80	20	-
Trade	99	1	88	12	-
Hotels and restaurants	100	-	90	10	-
Transport, storage and communications	99	1	93	7	-
Finance	98	2	93	7	-
Business activities	98	2	84	16	-
Public administration and defence	-	-	100	..	..
Education	100	..	100	..	..
Health and social services	100	..	100	-	-
Community, social and personal service activities	100	..	99	1	-
Other services	100	1	90	10	-

Source:
UNCTAD, *World Investment Report 2004: The Shift Towards Services*, United Nations publication, Sales No. E.04.II.D.36, table III.2.

Table A.10.

Distribution of stock of foreign direct investment in services by industry, 1990 and 2002

	Percentage						
	1990			2002			
Sector/industry	Developed countries	Developing countries	World	Developed countries	Developing countries	Central and Eastern Europe	World
Inward FDI stock							
Total services	100	100	100	100	100	100	100
Electricity, gas and water	1	2	1	3	4	6	3
Construction	2	3	2	1	3	5	2
Trade	27	15	25	20	13	21	18
Hotels and restaurants	3	2	3	2	2	2	2
Transport, storage and communications	2	8	3	11	10	24	11
Finance	37	57	40	31	22	29	29
Business activities	15	5	13	22	40	10	26
Public administration and defence	0	0	0	0	0	0	0
Education	0	0	0	0	0	0	0
Health and social services	0	0	0	0	0	0	0
Community, social and personal service activities	2	0	1	2	0	1	2
Other services	10	8	9	2	3	2	2
Unspecified tertiary	2	1	2	6	2	0	5
Outward FDI stock							
Total services	100	100	100	100	100	100	100
Electricity, gas and water	1	0	1	2	0	2	2
Construction	2	2	2	1	2	2	1
Trade	17	16	17	10	12	17	10
Hotels and restaurants	1	0	1	2	2	0	2
Transport, storage and communications	5	4	5	11	7	18	10
Finance	48	62	48	35	22	39	34
Business activities	6	11	6	34	54	19	36
Public administration and defence	0	0	0	0	0	0	0
Education	0	0	0	0	0	0	0
Health and social services	0	0	0	0	0	0	0
Community, social and personal service activities	0	0	0	0	0	0	0
Other services	13	5	13	2	2	2	2
Unspecified tertiary	6	0	6	3	0	0	3

Source:

UNCTAD, *World Investment Report 2004: The Shift Towards Services*, United Nations publication, Sales No. E.04.II.D.36, table III.1.

كيفيـة الحصـول على منشـورات الأمـم المتحـدة

يمكن الحصول على منشـورات الأمم المتحـدة من المكتبات ودور التوزيع في جميع أنحـاء العالـم . استعلـم عنها من المكتبة
التي تتعامـل معها أو اكتـب إلى : الأمـم المتحـدة ، قسـم البيـع في نيويـورك أو في جنيف .

如何购取联合国出版物

联合国出版物在全世界各地的书店和经售处均有发售。请向书店询问或写信到纽约或日内瓦的
联合国销售组。

HOW TO OBTAIN UNITED NATIONS PUBLICATIONS

United Nations publications may be obtained from bookstores and distributors throughout the
world. Consult your bookstore or write to: United Nations, Sales Section, New York or Geneva.

COMMENT SE PROCURER LES PUBLICATIONS DES NATIONS UNIES

Les publications des Nations Unies sont en vente dans les librairies et les agences dépositaires
du monde entier. Informez-vous auprès de votre libraire ou adressez-vous à : Nations Unies,
Section des ventes, New York ou Genève.

КАК ПОЛУЧИТЬ ИЗДАНИЯ ОРГАНИЗАЦИИ ОБЪЕДИНЕННЫХ НАЦИЙ

Издания Организации Объединенных Наций можно купить в книжных магазинах
и агентствах во всех районах мира. Наводите справки об изданиях в вашем книжном
магазине или пишите по адресу: Организация Объединенных Наций, Секция по
продаже изданий, Нью-Йорк или Женева.

COMO CONSEGUIR PUBLICACIONES DE LAS NACIONES UNIDAS

Las publicaciones de las Naciones Unidas están en venta en librerías y casas distribuidoras en
todas partes del mundo. Consulte a su librero o diríjase a: Naciones Unidas, Sección de Ventas,
Nueva York o Ginebra.

Litho in United Nations, New York
05-20562—January 2005—4,835
ISBN 92-1-109148-9

United Nations publication
Sales No. E.05.II.C.2